M000205059

In the Bleak Midwinter

Through Advent and Christmas with Christina Rossetti

In the Bleak Midwinter

*Through Advent and Christmas with
Christina Rossetti*

Rachel Mann

CANTERBURY
PRESS

Norwich

© Rachel Mann 2019

First published in 2019 by the Canterbury Press Norwich
Editorial office
3rd Floor, Invicta House
108–114 Golden Lane
London EC1Y 0TG, UK
www.canterburypress.co.uk

Canterbury Press is an imprint of Hymns Ancient & Modern Ltd
(a registered charity)

Hymns Ancient & Modern® is a registered trademark of Hymns
Ancient & Modern Ltd
13A Hellesdon Park Road, Norwich,
Norfolk NR6 5DR, UK

All rights reserved. No part of this publication may be reproduced,
stored in a retrieval system, or transmitted,
in any form or by any means, electronic, mechanical,
photocopying or otherwise, without the prior permission of
the publisher, Canterbury Press.

The Author has asserted her right under the Copyright, Designs and
Patents Act 1988 to be identified as the Author of this Work

British Library Cataloguing in Publication data

A catalogue record for this book is available
from the British Library

978 1 78622 162 9

Typeset by Regent Typesetting

Contents

Introduction

Morning and evening
Maids heard the goblins cry:
'Come buy our orchard fruits,
Come buy, come buy:
Apples and quinces,
Lemons and oranges,
Plump unpecked cherries,
Melons and raspberries,
Bloom-down-cheek'd peaches,
Swart-headed mulberries,
Wild free-born cranberries,
Crab-apples, dewberries,
Pine-apples, blackberries,
Apricots, strawberries;—
All ripe together
In summer weather,—
Morns that pass by,
Fair eves that fly;
Come buy, come buy ...'

Advent is traditionally a season of repentance and prayerful discipline. Readers might raise eyebrows that this book – which uses poetry to trace the rigorous power of Advent, as well as the joy of Christmas – begins with lines from Christina Rossetti's most ravishing and voluptuous poem 'Goblin Market'. Further, that rather than begin with her most famous devotional poem, from which this book takes its title, I begin with lines that show Rossetti in fantastical and secular mode.

'Goblin Market' might seem very far from this book's titular poem (properly called 'A Christmas Carol') whose themes of Christmas joy and intimacy are framed in taut and restrained lines:

In the bleak mid-winter[1]
   Frosty wind made moan,
Earth stood hard as iron,
   Water like a stone;
Snow had fallen, snow on snow,
   Snow on snow,
In the bleak mid-winter
   Long ago.

Our God, Heaven cannot hold Him
   Nor earth sustain;
Heaven and earth shall flee away
   When He comes to reign:
In the bleak mid-winter
   A stable-place sufficed
The Lord God Almighty
   Jesus Christ.

Enough for Him whom cherubim,
   Worship night and day,
A breastful of milk
   And a mangerful of hay;
Enough for Him whom angels
   Fall down before,
The ox and ass and camel
   Which adore.

Angels and archangels
   May have gathered there,
Cherubim and seraphim
   Thronged the air,
But only His mother
   In her maiden bliss

Worshipped the Beloved
  With a kiss.

What can I give Him,
  Poor as I am?
If I were a shepherd
  I would bring a lamb,
If I were a wise man
  I would do my part,—
Yet what I can I give Him,
  Give my heart.

However, I can think of no better place to start a book on the
joys, tensions and complexities of Advent and Christmas devo-
tions than Rossetti's extraordinary words of excess in 'Goblin
Market'. It is a poem that, nearly 160 years on from its original
publication in 1862, has lost none of its power to seduce and
tease. A friend and colleague at Manchester Metropolitan Uni-
versity – who has taught the poem for many years – says she
finds it impossible to read its list of fruits out loud without
feeling hungry. Such is Rossetti's grasp of the sensuous that her
poetry can be quite literally mouth-watering. Indeed, I would
go so far as to suggest that part of the power of her more
obviously religious poetry – often austere, careful and discreet
– is predicated on her profound understanding of the riches
found in desire. Rossetti is only able to offer religious poetry of
such demanding richness because she understands the depths
of our desire and the sensuality of the body. Indeed, as many
people have argued, if 'Goblin Market' can be read as a child-
like fable – and Rossetti suggested it should – it also contains
extraordinary readings of the Eucharist and of the power of
salvation, among many other things.[2]

You might find this all very exciting, but think it very far
from using Rossetti's religious poetry to negotiate the seasons
of Advent and Christmas. However, it is important leaven as
we come to engage with her writings in religious contexts.
Christina Rossetti was born on 5 December 1830 into a prominent

Anglo-Italian family. Casual readers of her work will almost certainly know that she is the sister of one of the nineteenth century's most prominent artists and poets, Dante Gabriel Rossetti, and may wish to set her with the Pre-Raphaelite Movement of which Dante Gabriel was part. Christina, however, is so much more. In recent years, her deep Anglican faith has been reckoned as significant not only as a key to understanding her poetry of faith, but as valuable to a mature understanding of her secular verse.[3] Indeed, there are grounds for saying that in her mature poetry, one should not be too rigid in separating her poetry into the sacred and the profane. For, running through her writing and her understanding of the world – ecological, aesthetic, personal and political – is her Anglo-Catholicism.

In the Bleak Midwinter is, first and foremost, a book that is designed to accompany us deeper into mystery and faith. This is not the place to offer an account of the influence on her thought of what has variously been called the Oxford Movement, Tractarianism or Anglo-Catholicism. For now, it is simply worth acknowledging this: Rossetti was powerfully influenced by Keble's 'poetry of reserve' which held that poetry was especially fit to speak of God and, in essence, is the 'handmaid' of Christian belief. For the likes of Keble, the gift of poetry – when properly deployed – is to bring the believer ever closer to God and his Church.[4]

Christina Rossetti was most serious about her faith. From as early as 1844, she attended Christ Church, Albany Street, whose minister, William Dodsworth, was a dedicated follower of the Tractarian movement (and who later converted to Roman Catholicism in 1851). Here she would not only have imbibed the centrality of the Eucharist for Christian faith, but have been exposed to a vision of the liturgical year charged with meaning and power. The most transformational encounter came during Advent 1848. Rossetti heard the Apocalyptic sermons – 'The Signs of the Times' – preached at Christ Church by Dodsworth. Their impact was such that the poet never lost that sense of wonder and the expectation of the Second Coming of

Christ. Running alongside that encounter was one with Keble's poetry. In 1827 John Keble had published a book of poems, *The Christian Year*, that traced his devotional response to the liturgical year. While Rossetti's brother, William Michael, claimed that his sister thought nothing of Keble as a poet, her copy of Keble's *The Christian Year* was heavily annotated, and arguably taught her much about the way time and space can be constructed very differently from the mercantile, secular and consumerist world emerging in the nineteenth century.

It is here that it is possible to discern the real connective tissue that brings the Rossetti of 'Goblin Market' and 'In the Bleak Midwinter' together, and that gives the impetus and modus operandi for this book. Christina Rossetti wrote huge volumes of religious and secular poetry. It is helpful to remember that she wrote poems on Classical subjects as well as Christian; her vision was shaped by Italian masters like Dante, as much as by emergent Anglican pieties, and she wrote in Italian as well as in English. She lived through the emergent heights of the Victorian Empire (dying in 1894) as part of one of the most prominent artistic families in the land; if by 1872, when 'In the Bleak Midwinter' was published, her poetic attentions were increasingly and firmly fixed on devotional verse and subjects, she also had a rich cultural and personal grasp of life's realities. Not only had she experienced the limits of being a middle-class woman in a patriarchal culture, she had experienced significant personal ill-health and familial loss.

These factors count when we come to read her poems in a devotional context. In her vast body of poetry, there are, arguably, a surprising number of seasonal poems. From our perspective, that might not seem hugely surprising; even Anglicans of a low-ish liturgical taste are quite used to the fact that there are Seasons of Advent, Christmas, Lent and so on; with differing levels of vigour, these seasons are marked. In Rossetti's Anglican context, however, a book like Keble's *The Christian Year* was a powerful intervention. Just as that era saw the emergence of new attention on the Eucharist and the renewal of the Religious Life in Anglicanism (with which

Rossetti can claim personal connection), it saw a powerful recovery of what we might call 'divine time'. This notion that the year might be structured through a divine lens is reflected in her commitment to produce poems for various seasons and saints' days.

It is possible to be sneery about Victorian women's poetry of devotion, seasonal and otherwise. Rossetti herself was for large swathes of the twentieth century marked down as a writer whose poetry revealed only the invisible world of her faith. Her poetry, so often read in her day through the sexist category of 'poetess' and marked as interior, sentimental and fragilely feminine, was – until the superb feminist recoveries of the 1970s onwards – too readily dismissed as a moment in 'excess Victorian piety'. Through the dazzling work of feminist critics in the 1970s, 1980s and 1990s, Rossetti's work was revisited and reinterpreted, and her genius was recognized. However, her faith was often seen as something of an embarrassing adjunct to her poetical talent. Indeed, until very recently, little critical attention and praise was given to her more obviously devotional verse.

The premise of this book is that Rossetti's poetry – both secular and devotional – can guide its readers into a powerful encounter with God's 'time' and space, a time that resists secular, commercial ideas. Just as the medieval era structured time differently from the modern era,[5] Rossetti's poems reveal that we don't have to simply structure time and space according to secular pressures. Rossetti's social, cultural and political 'time', of course, was one in which the emergent mercantile and the mechanical was the 'king'. In Victorian times, the pressure was on to make and sell things as quickly as possible; this was the age when the train was emerging. Time was being reworked and re-experienced anew by rich and poor alike.

By the time Christina died in 1894, the telegraph, telephone and the combustion engine were beginning to reshape time yet again. The world was becoming very small and humanity's place within it – often read as part of a mechanical, manufacturing process – seemed to be becoming very insignificant.

Identity was increasingly being defined by mass production and mass consumption. Mass-production techniques made cheapish, but well-made consumer goods available to the British middle classes for the first time; Rossetti's refrain in 'Goblin Market' – 'Come buy, Come buy!' – was echoing around middle-class lives (and increasingly working-class ones too) like never before.

The nineteenth century saw the emergence of department stores which provided 'palaces' in which the 'fruits' of Empire – both literal and metaphorical – could be touted and tried. It is into that world that Rossetti's verse – so often mocked by early twentieth-century critics as sentimental and sweet – speaks. If her reputation suffered for much of the twentieth century, the work of feminist and Christian-feminist scholars has now seen her placed – along with Elizabeth Barrett Browning – at the top table of Victorian poetry with the more familiar male counterparts, Tennyson and Browning.

Should anyone question why we should bother reading and meditating on Rossetti's poetry during Advent and Christmas, I trust you begin to see why. Ours is a time when consumerism and conspicuous consumption have become the norm. Christmas – which, as a concept, has so dominated Advent in the popular mind that Advent barely registers – has become the defining focus for the consumption of 'stuff'. Advent – that great season of discipline, preparation and fasting – has become so lost that if it registers at all in the popular mind, it is as a kind of reverse of classic meanings of Advent. Modern secular Advent means treating oneself to 'foretastes' of the feast, with barely restrained glee. Advent calendars – as ways to mark time until the first day of Christmas – have evolved into structured paths of indulgence; and such calendars today include not only chocolate treats but sometimes gin, whisky, cheese and so on. At one level, this is all good knockabout fun; at another, it frames 'Advent time' as '(self-)indulgent time'.

Running alongside this is an environmental concern that these levels of consumption are unsustainable and pernicious for the small planet on which we depend; aesthetically, there is an increasing sense that excessive consumerism is empty and tasteless. Just like the fruits of the goblin men, our consumerist pleasures turn to dust in our mouths and cannot satisfy us. As Christians, we must take a fair share of the blame for creating conditions in which defining yourself by what you can afford to buy others (or oneself) are the norm. However, Rossetti's extraordinarily astute and astringent poetry – often ravishing in its discipline and surprise – is alert to all these issues. She – as much as any Christian of our time – wishes to reclaim a sense of God's time. The poems contained here testify to that. Rossetti treats Advent as a time of preparation, reflection and discipline with profound seriousness. In the poem 'Advent' she writes of 'our good things long deferred, / With Jesus Christ our Best.'[6]

However, she is not afraid of Christmas joy. She understands the relationship between preparation and receiving the greatest gift of all, Christ himself. The power and shape of gift is a presiding theme of this book, and of the poem 'In the Bleak Midwinter' itself. This poem's key questions include, 'In what sense is the God-child actually gift?' and 'How can it be gift, at all?' The poem throws us into a scene at once familiar and strange – 'the bleak mid-winter'. We are in a world cold and moaning and bleak. It is a world in need. And who comes to dwell with us? 'Our God'. It is wonderful news, and yet disturbing and subversive. For this God – too great for heaven and earth – enters our world as a baby born in a stable.

Ultimately, 'In the Bleak Midwinter' is clear that – at the profoundest level – the arrival of a divine baby among us is gift, even in the bleak exposed world the poem constructs. Yet, how can that be? Part of the modus operandi of this book is to explore answers to that question. It seeks to follow the path to Bethlehem and beyond, in search of blessing and gift and joy, always held in a proper tension. This tension knows – as Rossetti knew – that there is always yet more; that as we encounter the Advent promise and the Christmas gift we only ever hold a partial vision of the World-Yet-To-Come, the Kingdom. We are called to speak of it, but carefully, discreetly and tenderly. It is a vision shaped through God's disturbing, wondrous and comforting time and space, which defines all in all, and ultimately calls us to make a response, at once corporate and also personal:

> What can I give Him,
>   Poor as I am?
> If I were a shepherd
>   I would bring a lamb;
> If I were a wise man
>   I would do my part;
> Yet what I can I give Him,
>   Give my heart.

How to Use this Book

In my experience, offering 'instructions for use' has limited value. Whether one is talking about assembling a piece of furniture, using a gadget, taking medicine or, indeed, reading how to use a book, most people simply ignore the instruction sheet. All they want is the 'headlines' and they only go back to the instructions when something goes wrong or 'goes weird'. For the most part, this human tendency does not lead to catastrophe, except perhaps in that case of wanton use of very dangerous gadgetry or the taking of 'moste potente potions'. In the case of *In the Bleak Midwinter*, a reader's decision to dive in and sample 'the wares' – as the goblins in 'Goblin Market' might put it – is unlikely to be disastrous. Unlike Laura in 'Goblin Market', should one brazenly luxuriate in Rossetti's poetry it is unlikely that one's hair shall lose its lustre or one's body wither (though if it does, I hope you do not bring a law suit against this book or me). Ultimately, each reader must find a way to read and pray that works for them.

At the same time, reading instructions can ultimately save headaches and irritations, especially when one is assembling a coffee table from a noted Swedish furniture retailer. There is value in being attentive to the way this book has been assembled. If the wares on offer here are not as dangerous as those offered by goblin men, poetry is potent, flavoursome and life-altering stuff. Considerable care has been given to the selection of poems offered in the book. Equally, they have been ordered with thought. Most significantly, I've sought to offer Rossetti's poems in the register of generous and attentive grace. I've sought not only to be kind to how these poems structure the seasons, but to invite the reader to consider how the moods and gestures in Rossetti's poems relate to one another. Poems must be able to stand alone, and yet – so often – they sing so very differently when they sit beside one another. I hope that my arrangement of these poems allows them not only to sing unexpected melodies, but to suggest secret harmonies.

Christina Rossetti's *The Complete Poems* (London: Penguin, 2005 (2001)) runs (with index) to over 1,000 pages. It is a vast, door-stopper of a book. To select 40-odd poems for this collection represents a fair task in itself. I say this not so much to crave your indulgence (though, like most writers, I should gratefully receive it), but to remind you that my selection is almost unavoidably idiosyncratic, limited and partial.

In short, serious scholars of Rossetti are likely to be disappointed or frustrated by some of my selections; casual readers may be surprised by my willingness to go beyond the devotional 'script' set by a book like this. As I indicated in the Introduction, I'm unconvinced by claims that one should make too sharp a distinction between the secular and the religious dimensions of Rossetti's poetry. One can only comprehend the sacred and profane alongside each other – one cannot take seriously what takes place in the Temple without a relationship with what lies beyond. On the evidence of her poetry, Rossetti had no fear of what lay outside the Temple. Nor should we. However, I do ask your forgiveness when my academic interest in her poetry unhelpfully dominates my attempt to offer sympathetic religious readings, and vice versa. It is the price exacted by reading a book written by someone who – as priest, hack and scholar – is (as northern friends might describe it) 'neither summat nor nowt'.

I hope that many of you reading this book treat it as a kind of 'poem a day' workbook. There is nothing wrong with workbooks. Indeed, there is something in the notion of the 'workbook' that connects us with the world of Christina Rossetti. Hers was a world where middle-class women were prevented from many of the activities we would now associate with the concept of 'work', and in which their 'work'

– sewing, embroidery, even their poetry – could be devalued as second-rate. To bring a 'workbook' mentality to bear on this book may encourage us to continue that process of reclaiming 'women's work' as a space of creative, potentially subversive, imagination.

Furthermore, work and craft are essential to both a life of prayer and making poems. There is discipline in both and, as I'm led to believe by those who are in the know, all Christians are supposed to be disciples these days; at the very least, we are supposed (to use that ugly American formulation) to be 'discipled'. As to how one might read the individual poems on offer, that is another matter. I am regularly told that no one reads poetry any more. This may or may not be true. One approach you might consider is to offer the poems the kind of prayerful attention one offers Scripture texts. Lectio Divina bears immense surprise when practised on biblical texts; such a mentality might do little harm and reap great good when applied to poems.

Poetry rarely offers up its gifts on first reading. I want to encourage you to avoid the (in my view) badly taught school idea that poems are like puzzles and we need to 'solve' each poem's 'code'. Ezra Pound's claim that 'poetry is the news that remains news' is closer to the mark. The freshness of Rossetti's poems lies in their possibilities of nuance and the new; we are not necessarily in search of their secrets, solved with a special key, but being invited into mystery. Rossetti's Christian faith – shaped as it was by Anglo-Catholic devotion – was not afraid of mystery; her devotional verse sought to offer ways of participation in God and, in my experience, that is typically a recipe for wonder, mystery and delicious bewilderment.

One structural point is worth considering before the reader proceeds to the poems: Advent is a curious season. Its true start, Advent Sunday, can fall on any date between 27 November and 3 December. In the selection of poems offered here, I've made the decision to act as if Advent Sunday falls on 1 December. In the Appendix, I offer supplementary poems that can be added in to the reading-scheme in years when Advent

Sunday falls earlier (simply add them in to the final week of Advent). The advantage of treating Advent Sunday as if it falls on 1 December is that it allows the reader to treat the four Sundays of Advent as days 1, 8, 15 and 22 of December, respectively. This means that a reader can disconnect the poems from the Sundays of Advent, strictly conceived, and follow the pattern of a classic 'Advent calendar' and begin reading them on 1 December. I trust this flexibility will be welcome to those who might like to read the poems alongside opening the doors on their Advent calendars.

Finally, a note on the commentary I offer on each poem. Each comment seeks to offer amplification rather than distraction. Should the reader simply treat this book as a 'selected poems' collection that would be enough – indeed, more than enough. Please feel at liberty to ignore my words of commentary. The treasure really is the poetry. Furthermore, I think it's only fair to offer a brief health warning: I've sought to avoid doctrinaire readings of Rossetti's poems. However, my own commitment to, and formation in, feminist understandings of nineteenth-century women's literature underlies my readings. That's what happens when one writes a PhD thesis on poetry from a feminist-Christian perspective. I don't apologize for this; rather, I want to own it. Part of the reason Rossetti is taken so seriously now is because of the work of women and feminist scholars. In a small way, I'm part of that tradition.

However, Rossetti was not in any modern sense a feminist. In a context where middle-class women's opportunities were constrained, she was by turns conservative and progressive. She used biblical ideas of woman's subordination to man as a reason for maintaining the status quo, while at other times she argued for female representation in Parliament. I trust that vignette captures the complexity of her personal, religious and poetic commitments in a context where representations of women and 'femininity' were fraught. However, no writer can control the effects of her writing, and all write into contexts. The potential readings of a poem escape the control of the poet who crafts it. I hope, however, that readers of this book will welcome readings of Rossetti's poems that are alert to questions of gender and sexuality as much as piety.[7]

Whether feminist or not, in my comments on her poems I've sought to offer my own often puzzled, often awed, response to Rossetti's capacity to ravish her reader even when her language is spare and restrained. Her craft is often magnificent, displaying a grasp of form that few contemporary poets might hope to emulate. However, she never loses sight of her deeper concern: God. Her poems are enacted in the 'in-between', as so much art, and Christian art in particular, must. As shall become clear, Rossetti's poems can be read as caught between wanting to speak and say as much as possible about the very life and riches of the world, while acknowledging the limits of language and the need for discretion in the face of wonder. I suspect no critic, especially one with gifts as limited as mine, can offer more to a poem than what it offers itself. Where my critical skills fail, I hope I leave Rossetti's poetic gifts to speak for themselves.

'Summer is gone with all its roses' – a place to begin

A book that proposes to use poetry to navigate Advent and Christmas should, perhaps, begin 'at the beginning' with a poem for Advent Sunday. However, I propose to begin 'before the beginning', with Rossetti's poem 'Sunday Before Advent', which closed the 'Some Feasts and Fasts' section of her final devotional collection, *Verses* (1893).

My decision to include it at the beginning of this book gives a neat and appropriate inversion of Rossetti's original idea. It reminds us of the cyclical nature of God's time and the truth that, as Eliot famously suggested, beginnings are simultaneously ends, and ends are beginnings. Humans are trained from infancy to divide their lives and purposes into years; Christians, no less than any other humans, are creatures of years. We live life 'directionally', as it were. However, Christian experience of the Church year and liturgical structure instruct us that life is also lived 'cyclically'. Each year we return to Advent and its invitation to be expectant and prepare for the fullness of God's Kingdom. Advent marks the beginning of the Christian year and to stand on its cusp, as 'Sunday Before Advent' does, is to be reminded that, above all things, we are children of God. The time and space we occupy is ultimately defined by God.

At the same time (sic!), those of us formed in the climate of Europe (and the UK particularly) know that our experience as seasonal creatures is also shaped by the changing scenes of nature. Even in these environmentally challenged times where seasonal shifts can seem harder to discern, we know that the seasons have different registers. 'Bitter for Sweet', included in Rossetti's first collection *Goblin Market and Other Poems* (1862), models these registers in simple and affecting lines:

Summer is gone with all its roses,
Its sun and perfumes and sweet flowers,
Its warm air and refreshing showers:
And even Autumn closes.

Yea, Autumn's chilly self is going,
And Winter comes which is yet colder;
Each day the hoar-frost waxes bolder,
And the last buds cease blowing.

The scholar Emma Mason has suggested that Rossetti is a poet who 'gentles' her audience into finding Grace through a recognition of the 'kinness of nature'.[8] Like Mason, I shall suggest that the pattern of our days is not found by setting up oppositions between nature and God, but in the relationships between them. For Rossetti, the story of the seasons is not a story beyond or outside God, but one that draws us deeper into the mystery. The world – fallen, hungry for renewal, marked by seasonal shifts, for sure – is charged still with the sacramental wonder of God. It waits, as the people of God wait, for the fullness of the Kingdom; just as poetry can draw the believer into deeper relationship with God, so can the patterns of the natural year. It is one reason why Rossetti is able to make such bold theological manoeuvres in her poetry, perhaps most especially in 'In the Bleak Midwinter' itself. The fierce sharpness of winter in that poem provides the crucible for the charge found in God's new life as a baby among us.

Before we arrive at Christmas, however, we must travel through Advent. Before Advent, it is also worth pausing and reflecting on the Sunday before Advent. For, on this Sunday, we wait on the brink – of the new liturgical year, of the New Creation, of the End of All Things. As the year tumbles towards its close, the blooms of summer and the fruits of autumn have withered, rotted or disappeared. It is a time of endings and a time of beginnings, and Christina Rossetti offers us words to go deeper. She prepares us for the Christian seasons to come.

Sunday Before Advent

The end of all things is at hand. We all
Stand in the balance trembling as we stand;
Or if not trembling, tottering to a fall.
The end of all things is at hand.

O hearts of men, covet the unending land!
O hearts of men, covet the musical,
Sweet, never-ending waters of that strand!

While Earth shows poor, a slippery rolling ball,
And Hell looms vast, a gulf unplumbed, unspanned,
And Heaven flings wide its gates to great and small,
The end of all things is at hand.

It is regularly claimed that Advent is a time for preparation. I don't want to dispute that. The question is: a time of preparation for what? The simplest and most obvious answer is Christmas, of course. During Advent, we are invited to strip away distraction and ready ourselves to encounter Christ again in the wonder of the incarnation. Rossetti's poem 'Sunday

Before Advent' is more direct and draws our attention towards another Advent theme: the Four Last Things (death, judgement, heaven and hell).

Rossetti begins and ends her poem with a simple, stark assertion: 'The end of all things is at hand.' For those who have lost sight of the sharp, startling power of Advent, her assertion might seem absurd. In our consumerist, commercialized world, our society has little appreciation of Advent as a time of sackcloth and fasting. It has rather been lost in the shininess of tinsel and the tinkling of pop music which wants 'every day to be Christmas'. Not so, Rossetti. She comprehends how Advent is a time to recognize we 'stand in the balance'; we 'totter' on the edge of a new creation: of the advent or arrival of Christ.

However, in Christian iconography, this is double-edged. On the one hand, Jesus has already entered our world as a historical figure. His incarnation is a fact of history. Yet, each year, as Advent arrives, Christians are invited to enter a time of anticipation and hope. It is not simply a matter of commemorating what has past, but honouring what is happening now, and what is to come. Thus, as we prepare to enter Advent, Rossetti reminds us that we are invited to prepare for Christ's return or Second Coming in glory. The imminent prospect of the Second Coming brings us into the orbit of the Four Last Things: death, heaven, hell and judgement. Advent, then, is – as this poem makes clear – a time of awe and wonder: Earth (with all its implications of limitation, 'flesh', 'sin' and wintry retreat from fecundity) is revealed in its poverty. It is 'a slippery rolling ball', while 'Hell looms vast, a gulf unplumbed, unspanned, / And Heaven flings wide its gates to great and small.'

'The end of all things is at hand.' For readers whose taste in poetry or rhetoric doesn't extend to the 'post-apocalyptic', this poem may seem unnecessarily dramatic. Yet, its speaker draws our attention to the way Christians participate in God's time and space. When Rossetti was alive, the Anglican Church – under the influence of Keble and those seeking to recover the deep language and traditions of Christianity – was in the process of rediscovering the power of the Christian liturgical year. The seasonal potential of the *Book of Common Prayer* was reinvigorated. For us – even those of us with 'low' liturgical tastes – the rhythms and seasons of the liturgical year are more clearly present. We structure our year as much through sacred time as through secular time.

The season of Advent signals the start of the new Christian and liturgical year. When Rossetti writes 'The end of all things is at hand', she speaks into our liturgically shaped lives as much as into eschatological reality. The old year is about to die and the new one is about to begin. When she writes 'O hearts of men, covet the unending land! / O hearts of men, covet the musical, / Sweet, never-ending waters of that strand!', she – in admittedly non-inclusive language – invites us to shape our desire around God's promises. The promise of the saviour is at hand; the promise of a new heaven and new earth approaches; a new year shaped by God's time approaches. It is a time of anticipation, hope and awe. It promises to disrupt us with the shock of glory; it will startle us away from our secular obsessions. God in Christ draws nigh.

In recent years, those of us in the more Catholic wing of the Church have, arguably, rather lost sight of what this poem suggests when it says 'The end of all things is at hand'. Why? Because we've adopted the feast of Christ the King on the last Sunday before Advent, rather than stick with the *Book of Common Prayer*'s structure. Even if we claim that Christ the King – a festival introduced in 1925 by Pope Pius XI – gestures towards the end-times, it tends to draw our attention towards Christ's kingship rather than the end of the liturgical year. Perhaps Rossetti's language chimes rather better with the old *Book of Common Prayer* collect for the Last Sunday Before Advent: 'Stir up, we beseech thee, O Lord, the wills of thy faithful people; that they, plenteously bringing forth the fruit of good works, may of thee be plenteously rewarded; through Jesus Christ our Lord. Amen.' In popular parlance, the last Sunday before Advent has become known as 'Stir-Up Sunday', associated with the twee practice of stirring and preparing the

Christmas Pudding. However, the notion of being 'stirred up' by God for God is a sharper and potentially more disruptive one. At the very least, as Rossetti indicates in 'Sunday Before Advent', we should prepare ourselves to be 'stirred up' by the God in whom all beginnings are found and all ends may be sought. 'The end of all things is at hand.' Advent is about to begin.

The First Week of Advent

'In the Bleak Midwinter'

Advent Sunday

Advent Sunday

Behold, the Bridegroom cometh: go ye out
With lighted lamps and garlands round about
To meet Him in a rapture with a shout.

It may be at the midnight, black as pitch,
Earth shall cast up her poor, cast up her rich.

It may be at the crowing of the cock
Earth shall upheave her depth, uproot her rock.

For lo, the Bridegroom fetcheth home the Bride:
His Hands are Hands she knows, she knows His Side.

Like pure Rebekah at the appointed place,
Veiled, she unveils her face to meet His Face.

Like great Queen Esther in her triumphing,
She triumphs in the Presence of her King.

His Eyes are as a Dove's, and she's Dove-eyed;
He knows His lovely mirror, sister, Bride.

He speaks with Dove-voice of exceeding love,
And she with love-voice of an answering Dove.

Behold, the Bridegroom cometh: go we out
With lamps ablaze and garlands round about
To meet Him in a rapture with a shout.

Biblical scholars agree that the King James (KJV) or Authorized
Version (AV) of the Bible is not the most accurate translation

of the earliest Hebrew or Greek manuscripts. It is, however, often transportingly beautiful and is certainly one of the foundational texts for English. Along with the *Book of Common Prayer*, and the works of Shakespeare, the KJV has supplied a wide and wonderful range of phrases and idioms to the language. For a poet like Christina Rossetti, the language of the *Book of Common Prayer* and the KJV formed a deep substrate.

These riches are reflected in her striking poem for Advent Sunday. Rossetti begins with a line lifted from Matthew 25.6 in the KJV: 'Behold, the Bridegroom cometh ...' The reader is thereby taken directly into Scripture before Rossetti's acute poetic judgement amplifies and unfolds its riches. The word 'behold' is fascinating. It litters the KJV – it appears over 1,000 times – not only drawing the reader's attention to the visual dimensions of the Good News (Look! See! Encounter!), but also implying possession, belonging and preservation. That is, when Rossetti uses 'behold' she invites us to participate in the scene: 'behold' invites the reader to be captivated by what follows and discover themselves in the unfolding scene. This is no mere intellectual matter, but something that delves into our being. It is, in short, an invitation into the adventure of Advent.

After its striking first clause, the opening stanza unfolds in a reasonably familiar way. Its theme – the coming of the Kingdom of God in all its fullness, terror and wonder – is familiar Advent fodder. Rossetti's opening gambit draws our attention to Christ's parable about the Wise and Foolish Virgins. In this parable, the Kingdom is likened to a bridegroom who comes unexpectedly in the middle of the night and is met by ten virgins; five are prepared and five are unprepared. It is a parable that invites us to reflect on how prepared we are for the unexpected arrival of the Kingdom of God, of Christ himself. Rossetti speaks to a Church that – because it is called to be alert to the need to live in God's time and reality – should be prepared to go out with 'lighted candles and garlands' and meet the Lord 'in a rapture'. Her excitement is irresistible, but also challenging: how ready are any of us for this Second Coming, for the coming of the Kingdom in all its fullness? How ready are the faith communities to which we belong? Advent Sunday is surely a day to reassess and recommit to that calling.

It is in the following stanzas that Rossetti really shakes her readers up and demonstrates her theological and poetic acuity. People of faith should already be alert to the promise that the Kingdom will appear unexpectedly; Rossetti underlines just how startling that appearance may be. She says, 'It may be at the crowing of the cock / Earth shall upheave her depth, uproot her rock.' Here we are thrown suddenly into St Peter's denial of Christ. Rossetti disconcerts the reader by suggesting not only that she is as complicit as Peter in denying the Son of God, but that these denials are ongoing. Indeed, at the very moment of our ongoing denials of God, he might break through with divine judgement. At a time when so many decisions in the Church and elsewhere can seem driven by commercial and consumerist priorities, it is a shocking wake-up call.

Poetry has a profound capacity to play with time and space; it can bring the oddest juxtapositions into a simple and suggestive present. This is precisely what Rossetti does in the central section of the poem. She deploys both the language of the cosmic relationship between Christ and his Church ('the Bridegroom fetcheth home the Bride'), as well as leading us back into stories from the book of Genesis. For she suggests that the Church is like Isaac's bride, Rebekah. Arguably, she isn't simply suggesting that the Church is like the kind, generous and lovely Rebekah; here, Rossetti ties the story of the Church's future glory to the ancient stories of the Patriarchs.

Rossetti reminds us that in some traditional ways of negotiating the Sundays of Advent, the first Sunday is an opportunity to reflect on the Patriarchs – Abraham, Isaac, Jacob and so on. These stories remind us that these figures established the pattern of our covenantal relationship with God. Strikingly, it is Rebekah of whom Rossetti speaks – she represents our faithful, loving and open response to God. The men are sidelined; as we shall see when we explore other poems, including 'In the Bleak Midwinter', it is women's faithfulness that is central to the safe arrival in our world of the Christ-Child. There is a quiet subversiveness in her poetics.

More than that, Rossetti adds another layer of biblical richness to her vision of the Church's (and our) response to the love of Christ: the Bride is like 'Queen Esther in her triumphing, / She triumphs in the Presence of her King.' This is a startling move, implying that Christ's bride is like Esther, the great exiled queen, whose cleverness and cunning saves the Jews from annihilation at the hands of King Ahasuerus's adviser Haman. Here, then, is an image of the faithful bride-Church as a saving community – a place where female brilliance is celebrated.

Ultimately, the central focus of this communion between Christ and his Church is 'exceeding love'; these are two doves made for each other. The Bride is the mirror of Christ, seeing clearly and face to face. Rossetti reveals her masterly knowledge of the biblical text, in the phrase 'dove-eyed', a reference back to the Song of Solomon (1.15). Famously, it is claimed that doves are monogamous and even that some species mate for life. The use of the 'dove-eyes' phrase not only takes us into theological space, but intimates the deep, loving and natural synergy between Christ and us, his Church.

Appropriately, the poem returns to its beginning. In offering the refrain 'Behold, the Bridegroom cometh', not only does it indicate the way in which God's salvation occupies non-linear time and space, it also points to the ways we are caught up in a cycle of liturgical time: Advent Sunday returns afresh to mark a new season of waiting, hope and anticipation. As Rossetti's final stanza suggests, the challenge for us is to meet the possibilities of the season with fresh eyes. When she writes 'Behold, the Bridegroom cometh ...' for the second time, we do not meet that invitation as we did when it was first issued. We have been drawn deeper into the story and possibilities of the season. We are ready to begin. We are ready to behold. We are closer to receiving God with a rapturous shout. We are not simply those on the sidelines looking on; we are participants in the mystery of love.

Day Two

Dead Before Death

Ah! changed and cold, how changed and very cold!
  With stiffened smiling lips and cold calm eyes:
  Changed, yet the same; much knowing, little wise;
This was the promise of the days of old!
Grown hard and stubborn in the ancient mould,
  Grown rigid in the sham of lifelong lies:
  We hoped for better things as years would rise,
But it is over as a tale once told.
All fallen the blossom that no fruitage bore,
  All lost the present and the future time,
All lost, all lost, the lapse that went before:
So lost till death shut-to the opened door,
  So lost from chime to everlasting chime,
So cold and lost for ever evermore.

In 'Goblin Market', Rossetti explores the abiding symbolic power of fruit and fruitfulness. As she demonstrates in that poem, for all the mouth-watering array of fruits offered by the 'goblin men', not all fruit is nourishing or life-giving. This fascination with the possibilities of 'fruitfulness' – theological, personal, conceptual – is reflected in another poem included in the same collection as 'Goblin Market': 'Dead Before Death'. Here, as in 'Goblin Market', she explores the dynamics between the possibilities of fecund life and death; however, in this poem, rather than occupying fairy-tale space, we are face to face with an uncomfortable lyric voice negotiating age, barrenness and loss.

Death, of course, is one of the Four Last Things explored as a key theme of Advent. It is tempting to treat death at the cosmic or theological level, treating it as humanity's Last Enemy, conquered by Christ in the resurrection. We might wish to treat it as a sobering question-mark hanging over us all as we await the coming of the New Heaven and New Earth, as indicated in the Apocalypse of John. There is merit in this, but Rossetti's poem takes these cosmic issues and locates them in the personal and the particular. The speaker's voice is plaintive and reflects on what it means to live in the midst of death before the death of the person or the death of all things.

When Rossetti writes about 'the promise of the days of old', it becomes clear, then, that it is a poem of experience. The voice is one who has lost her youth and, with it, its presumed fecundity and potential fruitfulness. This is not necessarily to be read as a matter of fertility and childbirth, but it is one horizon to be considered. I am cautious about reading too much biography into any poet's work, but there is truth in assertions that, after suffering serious illness in relative youth and as marriage prospects faded, Rossetti had to come to terms with what it meant to be a woman who would never bear children. It is sorely tempting to read these lines about blossom that bore no fruit in terms of her bodily fecundity:

We hoped for better things as years would rise,
But it is over as a tale once told.
All fallen the blossom that no fruitage bore,
  All lost the present and the future time,
All lost, all lost, the lapse that went before ...

However, as the Advent pilgrimage begins, 'Dead Before Death' reveals other horizons. To read the poem in the context of Advent invites us to confront our own encounters with death, barrenness and failure. As the secular year dies, a new liturgical year arises: hope springs! However, this should not trump too quickly the facts of our own failed schemes and the troublous nature of life. To contemplate death, both literal and metaphorical, is as much the work of Advent as looking forward to Christmas joy or the promise of the fullness of life in the Kingdom. Rightly, we place the death of the old year or the frustrations of our hopes in the light of God's reality, but we should be foolhardy to dismiss the facts of our lives. The critic Diane D'Amico reminds us that 'throughout her life, Rossetti accepted the doctrine that after death the soul did not enter into its full heavenly reward but had to wait until the Second Coming of Christ'.[9] Yet, as this poem reveals, doctrine must be negotiated through life's flesh. The speaker of the poem knows this and invites us into a way of understanding that can only be known through experience.

Rossetti has sometimes been held up as an example of a morbid, gloomy Victorian theology. That is, as representative of a kind of self-indulgent 'pleasure' in meditating on misery, pain and failure. There is evidence for that claim in this poem, and to many modern eyes it may appear unduly miserable. However, I wonder if part of the challenge for modern readers during this Advent, as in other seasons, is to come to a more 'Victorian' treatment of death. Our culture (both Christian and secular), as I shall revisit repeatedly in my comments, has a troubling tendency to obsess over the 'wonder' of youth and vitality-without-end; it seems to have a terror of death, annihilation and judgement. Perhaps a willingness to look at 'death before death' might draw us more hopefully into the possibilities of both Advent and Christmas and, indeed, the Christmas hope itself.

Day Three

Advent (1851)

'Come,' Thou dost say to Angels,
    To blessed Spirits, 'Come':
'Come,' to the lambs of Thine own flock,
    Thy little ones, 'Come home.'

'Come,' from the many-mansioned house
    The gracious word is sent;
'Come,' from the ivory palaces
    Unto the Penitent.

O Lord, restore us deaf and blind,
    Unclose our lips tho' dumb:
Then say to us, 'I will come with speed,'
    And we will answer, 'Come.'

One of the key features of Rossetti's poetry is masterful use of repetition. She uses it to build intensity and rhythm. In this poem from 1851 (though unpublished in her lifetime), her bold and brilliant use of repetition is a signal of her talent. For, in poetry, it takes not only confidence but also talent to deploy this poetic device successfully. Indeed, as many people who have spent time in contemporary poetry and creative writing classes know, the repetition of words and phrases can be seen as a beginner's error. It can be marked down as a clumsy device that indicates a lack of attention to the possibilities of language or a sloppy attempt to create poetic effects. In short, repetition is risky.

In 'Advent', Rossetti uses the word 'come' as a series of anchors in the first part of the poem. It is not immediately clear whether Rossetti uses it as an invitational word or a command. Indeed, part of the pleasure of deploying this word lies in the riches of its ambiguous connotations. This pleasurable ambiguity is complemented by discovering to whom the instruction is issued: the invitation, the command, is initially issued to the angels and to 'blessed spirits'. These two groups represent 'creatures' at the beck and call of God; Christ might – as we hear in the Gospel accounts of his temptation in the wilderness – command angels to raise him up. However, in lines three and four there is a subtle shift in the nature of the command. It moves from the heavenly creatures to the 'lambs' of his 'flock'. In this shift we discover the nature of the call: it is to 'come home'. This call is made to 'little ones'; there is, then, tenderness here. Christ says 'come' and his voice is not imperious; it is invitational and relational. Crucially, his call is an invitation to come home, away from (by implication) the wilderness. This is Christ as shepherd and tender carer for God's flock.

This instruction to 'come' moves, then, from a potential command to that of a call: it is a calling home, issued – we discover – from 'the many-mansioned house'. This reference to John 14 ('In my Father's house there are many mansions') takes Rossetti's reader into a world where Jesus – in his 'farewell speeches' – talks passionately and lovingly to his disciples ahead of his betrayal. We begin to see ever more clearly how the invitation to 'come' is 'the gracious word'. It is not a brutal command issued by a tyrant or emperor; it is a statement of relationship among those whom – as Christ has it in those farewell speeches – are no longer servants and slaves, but friends. The grace lies in relationship.

The final four lines create a turn. Here the speaker addresses the God who calls, who invites the penitent. She asks to be restored to fullness of relationship. The words 'deaf' and 'blind' act as metaphors for separation. The final couplet brings out the intense urgency of the season of Advent: for, after Christ has graciously invited us to come and dwell with him in his

Father's House, the speaker's longing for full union calls Christ back towards us. She hungers for Christ to say 'I will come with speed' into a world of longing and need. Finally, we – not just the poem's speaker, but the faithful people of God – will make our response to the God who invites. In our turn, we will say 'Come'.

This poem takes us deep into the relational, community-focused realities of God and us. Not for nothing do we speak of our God as 'covenantal'; this is not a God who merely makes contracts, but one who makes promises and invites us to live on and in them. This relationship operates in the economy of desire. So often the Church has had a downer on 'eros', cheapening it to nothing more than sexual desire. While there is surely nothing wrong with sex or sexual desire in themselves – indeed, in their place, they're rather wonderful – erotic desire runs far more richly through both our individual bodies and the body of Christ. The world itself is made in and through desire. Advent is a season when we appropriately meditate on these longings for fulfilment; it invites us, as Rossetti's poem does, into profound reflections on the dynamic and interlinked possibilities of God's desire for us, embedded in our bodies and souls. The question is: are we bold enough to do so?

Day Four

A Bruised Reed Shall He Not Break

I will accept thy will to do and be,
    Thy hatred and intolerance of sin,
    Thy will at least to love, that burns within
      And thirsteth after Me:
So will I render fruitful, blessing still
    The germs and small beginnings in thy heart,
    Because thy will cleaves to the better part.—
      Alas, I cannot will.

Dost not thou will, poor soul? Yet I receive
    The inner unseen longings of the soul,
    I guide them turning towards Me; I control
      And charm hearts till they grieve:
If thou desire, it yet shall come to pass,
    Tho' thou but wish indeed to choose My love;
    For I have power in earth and heaven above.—
      I cannot wish, alas!

What, neither choose nor wish to choose? and yet
    I still must strive to win thee and constrain:
    For thee I hung upon the cross in pain,
      How then can I forget?
If thou as yet dost neither love, nor hate,
    Nor choose, nor wish,—resign thyself, be still
    Till I infuse love, hatred, longing, will.—
      I do not deprecate.

Many critics claim that the dramatic monologue is a Victorian invention. E. Warwick Slinn claims that 'the dramatic monologue is arguably the flagship genre of Victorian poetry'.[10] Despite familiar assertions that the dramatic monologue was 'developed simultaneously but independently by Tennyson and Browning during the 1830s',[11] Isobel Armstrong claims it is a form that might plausibly be considered to be 'invented' by women.[12]

Rossetti was not a noted user of dramatic monologue, and whether 'A Bruised Reed' quite counts as dramatic monologue may be moot. What is intriguing is how Rossetti weaves together biblical texts and tropes into the performed voice of Christ. This first-person poem is bold and daring and profoundly risky: in a Victorian devotional context, to dare to speak in the voice of Christ might even have been read as disrespectful to the Divine. Indeed, if scholars are correct about dramatic monologue as a form, it might be seen as interrogating the very 'self' of Christ himself. Whether that has traction or not, the use of the first person for Christ also indicates the intense passion of Rossetti's connection with him; this monologue dives deep into biblical and theological readings of Christ's faithfulness and love. In its tender, sincere presentation of his obedience to the Father, this poem invites its readers into a closer, more intense relationship with God.

It may surprise some readers that I've chosen a Rossetti poem that seems to focus on the Passion of Jesus rather than Advent or his Nativity. 'A Bruised Reed' is redolent with the language of passion: it speaks of accepting 'thy will', which immediately takes the reader into the Garden of Tears, Gethsemane, where Christ's obedience and resolve were 'tested'. The voice, too, is mature, adult and reflective. This is the voice of experience rather than innocence. However, as I've suggested elsewhere, when we enter Rossetti's spiritual and theological universe, we must be alert to the way Christ's central narrative flows and interleaves: Nativity gestures towards Passion, death towards life, and eternity is woven into the present. In short, Rossetti's poetics are unafraid of the riches of God's time in which the

Kingdom is here and yet to come; where Christ's salvation is complete and yet breaking in.

How can we participate in this first-person poem? One of the most powerful prayer practices found in the *Exercises of St Ignatius of Loyola* is what is commonly known as 'imaginative contemplation'. This practice entails taking a passage of Scripture, say, and imaginatively exploring its possibilities. In that practice one dares to participate in the biblical 'drama' as one of the characters, perhaps even as Christ himself. I wonder if 'A Bruised Reed' offers poetic space for the reader's participation in Rossetti's vision of Christ? At the very least, it offers us – as modern readers – an opportunity to add our wills to that of Christ as he models obedience to God:

> I will accept thy will to do and be,
>   Thy hatred and intolerance of sin,
>   Thy will at least to love, that burns within
>   And thirsteth after Me ...

None of us are called to be Christ. Thank God for that. However, I am tantalized – indeed mesmerized – by what it would mean for me, for any of us, to take hold of that burning love of God that Christ knew. In the midst of the Advent fast, I want to have the boldness to be open to God's thirst, to God's will to love. I wonder where it might lead should any of us dare be so bold.

Day Five

The Three Enemies

The Flesh
'Sweet, thou art pale.'
  'More pale to see,
Christ hung upon the cruel tree
And bore His Father's wrath for me.'

'Sweet, thou art sad.'
  'Beneath a rod
More heavy, Christ for my sake trod
The winepress of the wrath of God.'

'Sweet, thou art weary.'
  'Not so Christ:
Whose mighty love of me sufficed
For Strength, Salvation, Eucharist.'

'Sweet, thou art footsore.'
  'If I bleed,
His feet have bled; yea, in my need
His Heart once bled for mine indeed.'

The World
'Sweet, thou art young.'
  'So He was young
Who for my sake in silence hung
Upon the Cross with Passion wrung.'

'Look, thou art fair.'
 'He was more fair
Than men, Who deigned for me to wear
A visage marred beyond compare.'

'And thou hast riches.'
 'Daily bread:
All else is His: Who, living, dead,
For me lack'd where to lay His Head.'

'And life is sweet.'
 'It was not so
To Him, Whose Cup did overflow
With mine unutterable woe.'

The Devil
'Thou drinkest deep.'
 'When Christ would sup
He drain'd the dregs from out my cup:
So how should I be lifted up?'

'Thou shalt win Glory.'
 'In the skies,
Lord Jesus, cover up mine eyes
Lest they should look on vanities.'

'Thou shalt have Knowledge.'
 'Helpless dust!
In Thee, O Lord, I put my trust:
Answer Thou for me, Wise and Just.'

'And Might.'—
 'Get thee behind me. Lord,
Who hast redeem'd and not abhorr'd
My soul, oh keep it by Thy Word.'

This triptych of poems examines Advent themes of attach-
ment, attention and distraction. It also demonstrates the taut,
unexpected possibilities in Rossetti's poetics. For, if she has

often been read as sentimental and conventional, here we find her using poetic form to break open emotional and intellectual possibilities. Leaving aside the devotional content, if this poem had been written by a twentieth-century experimental poet it would arguably have been designated as 'modernist' rather than 'traditional'.

Each poem engages with a theme deeply embedded in Christian discourse: the Flesh, the World and the Devil. One of the things that the Catholic spiritual tradition has successfully brought to the forefront is the question of 'attachment': which attachments – worldly, material and, indeed, spiritual – distract us from growing ever more into the likeness of Christ? This is a pressing question in every season of Christian formation, but especially during the season of Advent. If we are preparing ourselves to encounter Christ once again, what gets in the way? Rossetti takes us to the three traditional enemies of the soul, enemies that arguably act as a shadow to the Trinity. I mean not so much that Flesh, World and Devil are direct analogues of Father, Son and Holy Spirit, but that when we lose sight of our primary orientation in God, the Trinity, we fall into a kind of shadow represented by those other terms.

In each poem, Rossetti acknowledges and meets the attractions and attachments generated by those things that separate us from our true life in God. Words that signal a path to separation are cried out – 'Look, thou art fair', 'Sweet, thou art weary', 'Thou shalt win Glory', and so on – and are met with words of faith, hope and trust. She thereby expands on the Litany found in the *Book of Common Prayer*, in which the petition '… from all the deceits of the world, the flesh, and the devil' is met with 'Good Lord, deliver us.'

Rossetti frames her poetic responses to the Flesh, the World and the Devil using a 'call-and-response' structure. The 'cantor' speaks out of a voice of temptation and calls forth language of resistance. We are held in an endless poetic present, in which she presses home the urgency not only of temptation and sin, but of unhesitating response. In the ordinary rub of life, few of us have the wit, focus or holiness to make the kind of responses offered by Rossetti's speaker/s. We are not like Christ in the wilderness, presented with temptation, but readily able to find words of hope and resistance in the midst of our hunger and thirst.

Rossetti, however, stages a series of concentrated temptations and responses in these poems. Many of the pressure points delineated by Rossetti seem, to me, as contemporary as they ever were: the way she has 'Flesh' address its 'victim' using the affectionate diminutive 'sweet' is especially telling. It underlines the compromised relationships most of us have with our bodies. Equally, the temptations offered by the World and the Devil – to wealth, power, position and so on – are as old as the Bible and beyond. There is something reassuring about the changelessness of the ways in which life in a compromised and bust-up world makes fools of us all.

And yet ... as this poem explores beautifully, we can take hold of a language of liberation and resistance. The focal point for salvation always lies in God's abundance – in his nature as gift and grace. These poems show that, at the sharpest point of temptation, articulation of this truth matters. This trinity of poems not only offer striking poetic gestures, but constitute a series of prayers that may be offered in resistance to the crushing pressures presented during the season of Advent.

Day Six

Sweet Death

The sweetest blossoms die.
   And so it was that, going day by day
   Unto the church to praise and pray,
And crossing the green churchyard thoughtfully,
   I saw how on the graves the flowers
   Shed their fresh leaves in showers,
And how their perfume rose up to the sky
   Before it passed away.

The youngest blossoms die.
   They die, and fall and nourish the rich earth
   From which they lately had their birth;
Sweet life, but sweeter death that passeth by
   And is as though it had not been:—
   All colours turn to green;
The bright hues vanish, and the odours fly,
   The grass hath lasting worth.

And youth and beauty die.
   So be it, O my God, Thou God of truth:
   Better than beauty and than youth
Are Saints and Angels, a glad company;
   And Thou, O Lord, our Rest and Ease,
   Are better far than these.
Why should we shrink from our full harvest? why
   Prefer to glean with Ruth?

'Sweet Death' is a reminder of Rossetti's prodigious technical skill. In each eight-line stanza she presents a series of carefully ordered rhymes: the ending of line one rhymes with the end of line seven; two and three with line eight, and five and six with each other. There are other technical accomplishments. Consider lines three and four in the third stanza. Here, she deploys enjambment – the continuation of a sentence beyond the end of a line – to generate expectation and surprise. At no point do these technical displays feel awkward or arch. Rather, they combine to create an almost stately effect; there is a sense of quiet acceptance, a recognition that death, when placed in the economy of God's love and grace, can be sweet.

The poem begins conventionally enough. For, in natural terms, it is surely simply a fact that all blossoms, sweet and otherwise, die; death is part of the facts of earthly beauty. To live at all means that change is unavoidable; fragility, as the ancient Greek poet Pindar knew, is inscribed into life: 'Human excellence / grows like the vine tree / fed by the green dew.'[13] The speaker in 'Sweet Death' is reminded of this as she heads to church 'to praise and pray': she sees the flowers on the graves shed their beauty and witnesses their fragrance rise towards the heavens and pass away.

In this latter image, Rossetti – developing conventional images of graveyards and morbidity – begins to push pictures of death into something more striking. The implication is that the fragrance of the flowers is rather like the incense offered to God. If the speaker is 'seeing' this fragrance rise, she is seeing it with an inner eye of faith. It is an indication that death is very much not the end. If, as Psalm 105 (and Isaiah 40.6) reminds us, 'as for man, his days are as grass, like a flower of the field, he flourisheth,' none the less even the briefest blossom of life gestures towards the ultimate end of things.

As ever, with Rossetti, she is attentive to the cycle and pattern of life. However, it is always a pattern or cycle shaped in God's time. Her rhyming scheme invites the reader to consider the pattern of our days: each stanza cycles through the repeated, rhyming pattern. Images build that suggest that if youthful blossoms fall and die and nourish the earth from which they had their birth, these passing moments are held in a wider picture. Even death 'passeth by', as if it had not been. If a middle-class contemporary audience might struggle to appreciate our Victorian forebears' often intimate relationship with the imminence of death, surely Advent is a time to revisit its unavoidability and truth. Rossetti asserts that 'youth and beauty die'. So much in our culture seems determined to deny this truth, and yet even our fantasies of 'living forever young' are just that. Ironically, it is not Christianity that has a problem with death, but a consumerist culture that cannot even use the 'D' word. In a world where people are profoundly euphemistic about death – using words like 'passing' or 'gone on' – a poet like Rossetti is profoundly counter-cultural. Are we prepared to say that saints and angels are better company than youth and beauty?

Our desire (so often) is to be satisfied with a provisional and limited harvest of grace and love. This is the implication of Rossetti's reference to Ruth. Ruth – the outsider, the Moabite who follows her Israelite mother-in-law Naomi and adopts her faith – gleans at the edge of the fields owned by Naomi's relative, Boaz. It is a harvest of grace for – as the book of Ruth makes clear – Ruth is not entitled by right to glean these edge-lands. She receives permission from Boaz to do so. Rossetti's poem underlines that the graced harvest of Ruth is not the 'full harvest'. The terrifying, impressive implication of Rossetti's poem is that it is only in the embrace of death – of decay, of loss, of limit – that we have the promise of the full harvest of God's company.

It is unsurprising that we should be shocked and alarmed by this conclusion. It is not how secular, capitalist culture encourages people to think. However, death is unavoidable and each of us must come to some sort of viewpoint with regard to it. Rossetti reminds us that Christians encounter the 'God of truth'. This God invites us into a way of living that is so utterly open to the fragile that it always walks towards death rather than away from it. We do so not because we love death but because we seek after life. It is a way prepared to let go, rather than hold on. In John 12, Jesus says, 'unless a grain of wheat falls into the earth and dies, it must remain just a single grain; but if it dies it bears much fruit.' It is, like this poem, a verse worthy of pondering during a season of repentance and fasting.

Day Seven

A Portrait

I

She gave up beauty in her tender youth,
   Gave all her hope and joy and pleasant ways;
   She covered up her eyes lest they should gaze
On vanity, and chose the bitter truth.
Harsh towards herself, towards others full of ruth,
   Servant of servants, little known to praise,
   Long prayers and fasts trenched on her nights and days:
She schooled herself to sights and sounds uncouth
That with the poor and stricken she might make
   A home, until the least of all sufficed
Her wants; her own self learned she to forsake,
   Counting all earthly gain but hurt and loss.
So with calm will she chose and bore the cross
   And hated all for love of Jesus Christ.

II

They knelt in silent anguish by her bed,
   And could not weep; but calmly there she lay;
   All pain had left her; and the sun's last ray
Shone through upon her; warming into red
The shady curtains. In her heart she said:
'Heaven opens; I leave these and go away;
   The Bridegroom calls,—shall the Bride seek to stay?'
Then low upon her breast she bowed her head.
O lily flower, O gem of priceless worth,

O dove with patient voice and patient eyes,
O fruitful vine amid a land of dearth,
O maid replete with loving purities,
Thou bowedst down thy head with friends on earth
To raise it with the saints in Paradise.

The simple fact of the matter is that contemporary Western culture has travelled far from some aspects of Victorian pictures of death and devotion. If we, as a culture, have become obsessed with vitality, youth and endless health – a sentiment expressed in the famous German song 'Das wird ein Frühling ohne Ende' or 'Spring without end' – we have also become one in which a kind of tough, honest piety has increasingly become unavailable.

Arguably, the reader comes face to face with these differences in this pair of sonnets, especially in the first. And yet one should take care to be cautious. We should not overstate the self-effacing toughness and rigidity of Victorian self-understanding. The Victorian age, no less than ours, was a time of profound and rampant consumerism, especially among the English middle classes. The temptations to 'indulge' in the riches of Empire were almost boundless; this was the era when the department store came of age. This was an era when – for those with money – there was a cornucopia of delight on offer. If poverty was readily present beyond the comfortable confines of middle- and upper-class life, there were growing opportunities for the monied to become consumed by conspicuous consumption, as much as by the disease of consumption/ tuberculosis.

In the first of these sonnets, Rossetti presents us with a series of images and ideas that might seem a little bold even for the most pious twenty-first-century Christian. As a portrait of a person of faith it can strike us as almost ridiculous: here is a woman who 'gave up beauty in her tender youth', who

... covered up her eyes lest they should gaze
On vanity, and chose the bitter truth.

Harsh towards herself, towards others full of ruth,
Servant of servants, little known to praise,
Long prayers and fasts trenched on her nights and days...

Frankly, if one were to meet such a person in the twenty-first century – even, perhaps especially, among a religious community of nuns – one would, possibly, be inclined to run a mile. One simply would panic in the face of the depth of religious serious-ness or become suspicious of what sin they were concealing.

However, in the struggle to model the call of Advent, might one need a little more of the woman revealed here, rather than less? Rossetti lived through that period where forms of the religious life excised from England during the Reformation were restored. It might not be wise to overestimate the impact of Anglican sisterhoods on the life of the nation, but this was an era of extraordinary renewed interest in prayer, holy vows and practical service among middle-class women. Rossetti's sister, Maria, joined the Anglican Society of All Saints and both she and Christina gave time to serving at the St Mary Magdalene Home for Fallen Women in Highgate. If it is wrong to over-associate the portrait of devotion in these sonnets too readily with a nun, there is something suggestive about its representation of a consecrated life.

Perhaps such a consecrated life seems too middle class and 'genteel' – after all, in the poem one finds a woman who 'schooled herself to sights and sounds uncouth'. However, this poem's speaker displays a seriousness of intent to be learnt from. This is no self-indulgent 'schooling', but one shaped through a determination that 'she might make / A home' with the poor and stricken. This is a life lived in a willingness to let go of self-centred desire. This is a life where her 'own self' is forsaken. In one sense, the portrait is of one who comes into the place of forsakenness with Christ. I wonder what it might mean for any one of us, lay or ordained, religious or secular, to re-consecrate our lives to God during this time of Advent. It might be startling, in both its simplicity and its demands.

So many of us are children of privilege and comfort. I am. The challenges presented by this poem invite the reader to find, in her Advent longing, a preparedness to find hope in solidarity with the forsaken, indeed with Christ himself in his poverty and strickenness. The second part of the poem takes us to the point of death. Here, somewhat (melo-)dramatically, the subject of the poem says 'in her heart', 'Heaven opens; I leave these and go away; / The Bridegroom calls,—shall the Bride seek to stay?' The speaker in the poem shows faithfulness to God unto death. The Bridegroom Christ shall, in turn, be faithful unto her. If the affective excess of this scene can strike us as über-Victorian – like something out of Dickens – there is no doubt that, on its own terms, this poem is utterly sincere and serious:

Then low upon her breast she bowed her head.
O lily flower, O gem of priceless worth,
 O dove with patient voice and patient eyes,
O fruitful vine amid a land of dearth,
 O maid replete with loving purities,
Thou bowedst down thy head with friends on earth
 To raise it with the saints in Paradise.

There is another matter to consider. Perhaps this poem's form itself presents the greatest spiritual challenge to post-modern Christians and it is a challenge that might readily be overlooked. For this poem takes the form of a pair of sonnets. In choosing to invest 'A Portrait' with sonnet form, Rossetti insists the reader meditate on the possibilities of love. For that is the classical nature of a sonnet: it is a vehicle and model for love. That this poem comprises two sonnets indicates an intensification of that focus on love. For modern readers, even religious ones, it can be a struggle to see how a portrait of a self-effacing woman who is unenamoured with this world's temporary goods can take us deeper into love and its relationships. Yet that is what is on offer here. It presents us with serious, yet wondrous, challenges as we travel ever deeper into Advent.

The Second Week of Advent

'Our God, Heaven Cannot Hold Him'

Advent Two

Advent (1858)

This Advent moon shines cold and clear,
    These Advent nights are long;
Our lamps have burned year after year
    And still their flame is strong.
'Watchman, what of the night?' we cry
    Heart-sick with hope deferred:
'No speaking signs are in the sky,'
    Is still the watchman's word.

The Porter watches at the gate,
    The servants watch within;
The watch is long betimes and late,
    The prize is slow to win.
'Watchman, what of the night?' but still
    His answer sounds the same:
'No daybreak tops the utmost hill,
    Nor pale our lamps of flame.'

One to another hear them speak
    The patient virgins wise:
'Surely He is not far to seek'—
    'All night we watch and rise.'
'The days are evil looking back,
    The coming days are dim;
Yet count we not His promise slack,
    But watch and wait for Him.'

One with another, soul with soul,
   They kindle fire from fire:
'Friends watch us who have touched the goal.'
   'They urge us, come up higher.'
'With them shall rest our waysore feet,
   With them is built our home,
With Christ'—'They sweet, but He most sweet,
   Sweeter than honeycomb.'

There no more parting, no more pain,
   The distant ones brought near,
The lost so long are found again,
   Long lost but longer dear:
Eye hath not seen, ear hath not heard,
   Nor heart conceived that rest,
With them our good things long deferred,
   With Jesus Christ our Best.

We weep because the night is long,
   We laugh for day shall rise,
We sing a slow contented song
   And knock at Paradise.
Weeping we hold Him fast, Who wept
   For us, we hold Him fast;
And will not let Him go except
   He bless us first or last.

Weeping we hold Him fast to-night;
   We will not let Him go
Till daybreak smite our wearied sight
   And summer smite the snow:
Then figs shall bud, and dove with dove
   Shall coo the livelong day;
Then He shall say, 'Arise, My love,
   My fair one, come away.'

I can get a little over-excited about liturgy. In particular, I can become a little giddy about the idea of the 'Drama of the

Liturgy'. The phrase indicates how the Eucharist enacts, and therefore enables us to participate in, Christ's story. It is a reminder that liturgy is never mere words. When we participate in the Eucharist we participate in God's drama of forgiveness, sacrifice and redemption.

The notion of drama is worth keeping in mind when we place the liturgy in its seasonal contexts. Advent, as we often reiterate, entails watching and waiting; it entails being attentive to the Christ who is here and yet to come. We watch most especially for the Second Coming of Christ. Rossetti's poem 'Advent' demonstrates not only that she is a master of poetic form and has a rich understanding of liturgical gesture and movement, but that she has a dazzling grasp of drama in poetry. 'Advent' is a masterpiece of engagement, movement and drama. It enables its reader to participate deeply and richly in the watching, waiting and wonder of Advent.

In 'Advent', she presents the drama of salvation writ large. Here is a cast of characters drawn from 'End Times' central-casting: watchmen/watchers and 'patient virgins' gather together in the flickering light of night in anticipation of the coming of their Lord. Rossetti, with a masterly grasp of the intersections between divine and natural time, sets this drama on a 'cold and clear' December night. Her speaker acknowledges the longing for light embedded into a season where daylight is short and the night long. If, for some readers, this represents a Euro-centric reading of Advent (and Christmas) – as a season best read when located in a European wintry context – I have sympathy. Nearly 30 years ago, I had Christmas in Jamaica and – as my then-partner and I discovered – European rituals and ideas were exposed as contextually weak. While I'm happy to acknowledge that, it seems harsh to accuse Rossetti of excess Euro-centrism. Readings of ritual and liturgical season have to be located somewhere, because humans are the kind of creatures who are 'of' somewhere; anyone who has ever sought to keep the fast of Ramadan in a European summer context, where daylight lasts for nigh on 20 hours, will appreciate how that style of fast was unlikely to emerge in a European context.

I've already spoken of virgins and bridesmaids in my commentary on earlier poems. However, it's worth making some reflection on 'watchers' or 'watchmen'. If one wants to count oneself among those who wish to follow the Star of Christ towards Christmas and the New Creation, it would be foolish to ignore the call to 'alertness' and 'attention'. The call to faithfulness means the call is not an optional extra. Indeed, it is telling that one dimension of the 'character' of priesthood, rehearsed at all ordinations by the bishop, is the call to be 'watchmen' or 'watchers'. In the days when I helped prepare deacons for priesthood, it was the 'characteristic' of priestly ministry most were indifferent to. When asked to identify those dimensions of priesthood they were drawn to, they spoke of the pastoral or the proclamatory or presidential, rather than the injunction 'to watch for the signs of God's new creation'. However, perhaps the willingness to be still, be alert and look out for the *poeïsis* – or 'creativity' – of God in the world, perhaps precisely in those situations that are most uncomfortable and troubling, is the foundation of our pastoral call and action. Out of that attention comes both solidarity and transformative action.

It is in the watching and waiting for the signs – in the anticipation – that we are caught in the in-between of the old world that is passing away and God's new making or creation. The final two stanzas of Rossetti's poem capture the cusp of joy and weeping that signals the realm of new birth. On the borderlands of new life – of physical birth, but also as we prepare to enter a new territory, either literal or metaphorical (or both!) – we might hear cries that could be both laughter and tears:

We weep because the night is long,
  We laugh for day shall rise,
We sing a slow contented song
  And knock at Paradise.
Weeping we hold Him fast, Who wept
  For us, we hold Him fast;
And will not let Him go except
  He bless us first or last.

Weeping we hold Him fast to-night;
   We will not let Him go
Till daybreak smite our wearied sight
   And summer smite the snow:
Then figs shall bud, and dove with dove
   Shall coo the livelong day;
Then He shall say, 'Arise, My love,
   My fair one, come away.'

Day Nine

Vanity of Vanities

Ah woe is me for pleasure that is vain,
   Ah woe is me for glory that is past:
   Pleasure that bringeth sorrow at the last,
Glory that at the last bringeth no gain!
So saith the sinking heart; and so again
   It shall say till the mighty angel-blast
   Is blown, making the sun and moon aghast,
And showering down the stars like sudden rain.
And evermore men shall go fearfully
   Bending beneath their weight of heaviness;
And ancient men shall lie down wearily,
   And strong men shall rise up in weariness;
Yea, even the young shall answer sighingly,
   Saying one to another: How vain it is!

Few of us escape a bout of 'self-pity' at some point in our lives.
Perhaps there are some who are especially prone to it. I think I
may be one. At the very least, I am aware that I have something
of a narcissistic personality and can collapse into self-pity a
little too readily. I know some people create the impression of
formidable self-control. None the less, I struggle to believe that
anyone is fully immune to the 'woe is me' moment. We would
not be the fragile and bewildered creatures we are if we were
so immune.

   The context for 'Vanity of Vanities' pushes somewhat farther
than most the 'woe is me' moments (though, arguably, it still

belongs to the same species as regular encounters with self-pity). The context for this sonnet is Ecclesiastes 1, classically attributed to Solomon, the wise son of King David. Ecclesiastes opens with, 'Vanity of vanities, saith the Preacher, vanity of vanities; all is vanity. What profit hath a man of all his labour which he taketh under the sun?' The poem is grounded in a philosophically resigned attitude, shaped around a sense of world-weariness and dissatisfaction with the shadow-play of this world. From the point of view of eternity, the affairs of this world can all seem pointless. Indeed, Rossetti scholar Lizzie Ludlow indicates that when Rossetti composed this sonnet in the 1840s she was significantly influenced by a version of Platonism that commended an attitude of resignation.[14]

The sestet at the close of the sonnet repeats the word 'men' three times. It creates bleak effects. In the imaginative world sketched by Rossetti, 'evermore men shall go fearfully / Bending beneath their weight of heaviness'. Equally, the ancient 'shall lie down wearily', and the strong shall rise 'in weariness'. In this imaginary world, even the young will agree on the vanity of life. This contrasts strongly with the prophecies of Isaiah with which Rossetti's poem has some echoes. In Isaiah 40.30–31, the prophet suggests that although youths shall faint and be weary, and young men shall fall, they that wait upon the Lord shall renew their strength and rise on eagles' wings. In 'Vanity of Vanities', we find Rossetti in bleak mode. In a meditation on Ecclesiastes found in a later prose work, *Seek and Find* (1879), Rossetti acknowledges that in its conception 'Vanity of Vanities' 'amounts to so exquisite a dirge over dead hope and paralysed effort that we are almost ready to fall in love with our own desolation' (p. 272).

'We are almost ready to fall in love with our own desolation.' I find that an extraordinary and challenging sentence, whereby Rossetti reveals a depth of spiritual understanding that speaks into the nuances and shades of self-pity. If self-pity is certainly not to be confused with depression, there may be intersections. Equally, desolation intersects with depression. I have known periods in my life when I've negotiated the crushing absence of feeling that can be characteristic of depression and desolation. It is encouraging to know that these absences are known in the Christian tradition: St John of the Cross speaks of the Dark Night of the Soul and St Ignatius speaks of 'desolation'. Equally, one of the striking truths of the biblical texts is their honesty.

If it is the case that the classic shape of those biblical texts is to move from desolation or pain or brokenness towards hope and comfort, none the less this shift is predicated on the fact that this life can be a vale of tears. I find Rossetti's poem especially affecting, however, because – as she later acknowledged – it reveals how 'we are almost ready to fall in love with our own desolation'. We can be so seduced by the temptation to despair that we become infatuated by bleakness. For it is safe or known. As many know – and as I have commented on in other places[15] – the great philosopher Gillian Rose used a line from Staretz Silouan as an epigraph in her rigorously honest memoir, *Love's Work*: 'Keep your mind in hell and do not despair.' It is a salutary line for someone who wished to face death and cancer without cheap comfort. It might also be a complementary line to set alongside Rossetti's: that though we may find ourselves in hell or the vain emptiness of a life, we must resist the seduction of despair, the attractions of desolation. The challenge of Advent – terrific and almost impossible to embrace – requires it.

Day Ten

Winter Rain

Every valley drinks,
    Every dell and hollow:
Where the kind rain sinks and sinks,
    Green of Spring will follow.

Yet a lapse of weeks
    Buds will burst their edges,
Strip their wool-coats, glue-coats, streaks,
    In the woods and hedges;

Weave a bower of love
    For birds to meet each other,
Weave a canopy above
    Nest and egg and mother.

But for fattening rain
    We should have no flowers,
Never a bud or leaf again
    But for soaking showers;

Never a mated bird
    In the rocking tree-tops,
Never indeed a flock or herd
    To graze upon the lea-crops.

Lambs so woolly white,
    Sheep the sun-bright leas on,
They could have no grass to bite
    But for rain in season.

We should find no moss
In the shadiest places,
Find no waving meadow grass
Pied with broad-eyed daisies:

But miles of barren sand,
With never a son or daughter,
Not a lily on the land,
Or lily on the water.

As I write, a cold, dismal rain falls outside my window. It is December in Manchester, so that is hardly surprising. Manchester, after all, is called the 'Rainy City'. During the shortened days of December, there is much in our culture that has conditioned us to long for, if not expect, snow. So much of our cultural understanding of the days of Advent and Christmas has been shaped by the rituals and myths of our Victorian forebears (though Dickens's role in 'inventing' Christmas has surely been wildly exaggerated). Christina Rossetti herself deserves some blame, if that is the word, for our fantasies of December. In some ways, 'In the Bleak Midwinter' offers the acme of our European cultural representations of this season.

'Winter Rain' offers a different tenor. It may surprise some readers that I include it in this book, not least because it is not an obviously devotional poem. However, it explores both metaphoric riches located in the loam of (European) understandings of Advent, as well as inviting the reader to consider pressing environmental themes. For, if Advent is rightly understood in theological terms as a time of longing and preparation, it also chimes with the seasonal facts of a European/British winter. Winter presents graphic representations of our longing for bloom, new life and delight. In Rossetti's poem, it is 'every valley' and 'every dell and hollow' that drink deep of winter rain, quenching 'their' thirst in a time of seeming barrenness and famine. The very language here – dell and hollow – is suggestive of emptiness, in need of filling. Yet, in this bleak season of 'soaking showers' – drowned and desperate – lies the potential for 'buds to burst'. It is in winter rain that 'a bower of love' may ultimately be woven.

A bower of love. It is, as so often with Rossetti, an arresting phrase. A bower is a shady place in a garden, derived from the Old English for 'dwelling' or 'inner room'. Further back still, in Germanic languages the word suggests 'bird nest'. In Rossetti's poem, which begins in the drenching of winter rain – so often relentless and bleak – we find the possibility of branches in which birds may meet and love and renew the cycle of life. Truly this is 'fattening rain', another startling phrase. From the valleys and hollows flows new life and a dwelling-place for love.

For those of us of a theological bent, it does not take too much effort to let this image flow towards other images and ideas of the season: from the seemingly barren and bleak comes a bower of love in which God may dwell. In their study of women poets, Yopie Prins and Maeera Shrieber remind us that – in Old English – the word 'dwellen' means 'to lead astray', developing into 'tarry, stay in place'.[16] It is a suggestive idea. In the context of Christ coming to dwell with us, it suggests that he does so not as a fixed, safe entity, but as the one who goes astray from established meaning. The Word of God dwells with us as one who creates new poetic possibilities.

Placing a poem like 'Winter Rain' in the context of Advent allows fresh resonances for readings of both secular and divine seasons. Rossetti suggests that the bower in which nature's love may dwell is predicated on winter, on its rain and cold and barrenness. The new life of spring is held in the chill of winter. Equally, Advent offers a time of stripping away and reconfiguration. It presents its own bower – a space into which God may come and dwell beside us. This bower of love takes the form of Bethlehem, where Christ may be born among us. It is a space as tiny as a stable, as vast as the universe.

Day Eleven

The Lowest Place

Give me the lowest place: not that I dare
    Ask for that lowest place, but Thou hast died
That I might live and share
    Thy glory by Thy side.

Give me the lowest place: or if for me
    That lowest place too high, make one more low
Where I may sit and see
    My God and love Thee so.

Rossetti's devotional verse has often been treated by critics, both those sympathetic and those antipathetic towards her, with suspicion. It has been suggested that – compared to Gerard Manley Hopkins, for example – her religious poetry rarely achieves anything save a cloying sentimentality that destroys her gifts. 'The Lowest Place' – a poem that closes her 1866 second collection, *The Prince's Progress and Other Poems* – might be read through that lens: rather than achieving the quiet power of song, a poem like 'The Lowest Place' too readily reaches for a childish sing-song. Each reader must decide for herself or himself whether that particular criticism of Rossetti is appropriate, or whether, for example, it may reflect some gendered bias against the poetry of a woman of faith.

Personally, I have been on something of a journey concerning Rossetti's devotional verse. Where once I was inclined to read its sincerity as a red flag that signalled the decay of her gifts as she travelled towards middle age, I have slowly come to a different mind. As I've grown older and more settled in faith, I've become attuned to the simplicity and nuance that is embedded in her devotional words. If 'The Lowest Place' might readily be dismissed because of its conventional rhyming scheme and rhythms, I've come to appreciate the characteristic Rossettian tensions its two short verses contain.

Each verse begins with a request to God that verges on a demand: 'Give me the lowest place ...' I'm intrigued by this request. From a Christian point of view, there are sincere reasons why a disciple might ask for the lowest place in heaven or earth, in the Kingdom, or in the company of the saints. After all, Christ says, 'If any man desire to be first, the same shall be last of all, and servant of all.' However, the request itself, made boldly and without run-up (as it were), immediately suggests that the speaker has a firm grip on where she stands with God: she has a clear sense of herself and her limits. This is humility as self-awareness. The speaker comprehends her place in the world, rather than offering the false grubbing-around ('ooh, I am a worm') that often presents itself as humility. She offers a kind of spiritual 'antonym' of James's and John's request to sit on either side of the throne of Jesus.

However, immediately the reader is thrown into a Rossettian tension: the speaker issues her bold request, and yet when that is placed before the 'majesty' of God, she immediately recognizes that she lacks the worth or the character to even dare ask for the lowest place. For – again, contrast with James's and John's request of Christ, 'Grant us to sit, one at your right hand and one at your left, in your glory' – in Christ's disruptive, troubling Kingdom, the lowest place is the place of exultation. If this poem lacks the wild linguistic riches of some of Rossetti's writing, that does not necessarily damage its effects. The closing section of the second stanza is plaintive and deeply affecting, deploying irony to engage rather than to show off (as it so often is deployed today). The speaker acknowledges that if the lowest place is – ironically – still too high for her, it might be possible for her to approach this place by occupying 'one more low / Where I may sit and see / My

God and love Thee so.' I do not find this sickly or cloying. There is temerity in the speaker's seeming timidity; her self-abnegation may yet be rewarded with a curious exaltation. There is audacity in this request.

Rossetti was a woman who negotiated considerable personal and social struggles. At one level, she was a privileged middle-class woman, but she was also a woman in a culture that treated her as definitively second-class; in addition, she was a woman who negotiated significant ill-health and pain. Her family faced, as a result of the deterioration of her father's health, financial anxieties and, what with personal break-downs and the frustrations of love affairs, she did not live a straightforward life. Placed in the context of a life that was by turns relatively privileged and yet scarred by its own quotient of suffering, 'The Lowest Place' is not a self-pitying or self-indulgent poem. It indicates a simple, considered willingness to enter the ironies of authentic faith. It can speak to any one of us who, for the most part, are curious mixtures of privilege and pain; it can help us face the challenges of Advent with clear-eyed honesty.

Day Twelve

For Advent

Sweet sweet sound of distant waters falling
  On a parched and thirsty plain;
Sweet sweet song of soaring skylark, calling
  On the sun to shine again;
Perfume of the rose, only the fresher
  For past fertilizing rain;
Pearls amid the sea, a hidden treasure
  For some daring hand to gain;—
  Better, dearer than all these
  Is the earth beneath the trees:
  Of a much more priceless worth
  Is the old, brown, common earth.

Little snow-white lamb piteously bleating
  For thy mother far away;
Saddest sweetest nightingale retreating
  With thy sorrow from the day;
Weary fawn whom night has overtaken,
  From the herd gone quite astray;
Dove whose nest was rifled and forsaken
  In the budding month of May;—
  Roost upon the leafy trees;
  Lie on earth and take your ease:
  Death is better far than birth,
  You shall turn again to earth.

Listen to the never-pausing murmur
  Of the waves that fret the shore:
See the ancient pine that stands the firmer
  For the storm-shock that it bore;
And the moon her silver chalice filling
  With light from the great sun's store;
And the stars which deck our temple's ceiling
  As the flowers deck its floor;
  Look and hearken while you may,
  For these things shall pass away:
  All these things shall fail and cease;
  Let us wait the end in peace.

Let us wait the end in peace, for truly
  That shall cease which was before:
Let us see our lamps are lighted, duly
  Fed with oil nor wanting more:
Let us pray while yet the Lord will hear us,
  For the time is almost o'er;
Yea, the end of all is very near us;
  Yea, the Judge is at the door.
  Let us pray now, while we may;
  It will be too late to pray
  When the quick and dead shall all
  Rise at the last trumpet call.

We live in an age where, seemingly, life is celebrated almost as an end in itself. The advertising that surrounds and shapes us encourages us to drink deep of the well of life. There is an excessive and irrational devotion to adventure. We are supposed to have 'experiences'. Adverts aimed at people at every stage of life – from children who might like Disney through to older people who might prefer a cruise – emphasize the priority of creating memories and experiences that last. This hunger for experience is presented as a celebration of life itself, and perhaps it is. However, it might equally be a response to a world that feels deeply dehumanizing. Many workers are increasingly treated like machines, often – if media reports are to be believed – deprived of human rights to take proper breaks and holidays. This is the time of the 'gig economy' where people carry their offices around in phones and can – and do – work 24/7. They take work where it can be found and often that work does not supply enough money to have much of a life. Perhaps it is natural to respond to this dehumanization with a desire to find ways to enjoy life for its own sake; to gather up as many experiences as possible.

Rossetti's world was not necessarily as different from our own as we might imagine. It was a culture negotiating industrialized work and mechanization, as well as shifts in the meaning of what it meant to be a human being. This was a world in which human beings were discovering what it might mean to be secondary to other factors and forces: industry, evolution, and so on. This was a world where concepts of nature were being reworked. The idea that human beings might be 'secondary' rather than the crown of creation began to gain traction during the decades in which Rossetti lived. This was a world that demanded high levels of labour to service mass production rather than highly skilled artisans; it was a world where question marks were raised about the place of God and the Bible in emerging understandings of nature.

'For Advent' presents a characteristically Rossettian response to these questions about nature, God and what it means to be human. The poem evokes satisfying images, even sentimental and beguiling ones, only to subvert them by a preparedness to present the facts of death and decay. As ever, in our world where death cannot be spoken of, seen or faced, this willingness borders on the disturbing. Thus, 'For Advent' initially invites the reader into an almost arcadian world:

Sweet sweet sound of distant waters falling
   On a parched and thirsty plain;
Sweet sweet song of soaring skylark, calling
   On the sun to shine again;
Perfume of the rose, only the fresher
   For past fertilizing rain ...

If this is not quite a vision of Eden, it is a vision of a world where, as Isaiah 55 has it, 'ye shall go out with joy, and be led forth with peace: the mountains and the hills shall break forth before you into singing, and all the trees of the field shall clap their hands.' This is a land where the parched plain is satisfied and fertilized.

Cleverly, just as the reader is beguiled by these images, Rossetti's speaker quietly develops a deeper and subtler point. She says,

Better, dearer than all these
Is the earth beneath the trees:
Of a much more priceless worth
Is the old, brown, common earth.

This is intriguing. Does she mean that what really matters lies beyond the beauteously obvious? At one level, yes. This is a reminder that at the level of the 'natural', the blooming and blossoming of life is as nothing without a deeper layer sustaining it. However, Rossetti has still more in wait for us. The poem invites the reader not only to consider 'the natural', but to meditate on spiritually potent and religious dimensions of death. For, as the closing couplet of the second stanza claims:

Death is better far than birth,
You shall turn again to earth.

I suspect most people today would question the truth of Rossetti's assertion that 'death is better far than birth', even if all – whether of faith or not – would surely have to accept that all shall 'turn again to earth'. From a secular perspective, there is something gothic in Rossetti's claim – at least in its popular sense as gloomy and doomy! However, there is a theological challenge in Rossetti's claim. Few of us in the privileged countries of the Western world know the depth of pain or desperation that might lead one to assert that 'death is better far than birth'. Even when one faces times of profound strain –

as those who know chronic illness have – one often still asserts the priority of life over death, and rightly so.

So what might be her point? It may be twofold. First, death is unavoidably a feature of life and life truly lived; in addition to the ultimate end represented by death, living well entails existing alongside the many deaths embedded in life. I, like many feminists, want to retrieve the power of the 'natal'. We all need to learn to discover what it means to be creatures who are *being born*, rather than dying. Birth is beautiful in so many ways – we are so readily disarmed by the arrival of a baby – and I wonder what might happen to our understanding of being human if we could focus on birth rather than death. However, to be born is also to struggle and it is a throwing-out of the relative safety of the womb; it is a kind of death and death is a letting-go. The various 'letting-goes' of a life well lived are so many deaths, but arguably represent the necessary process of growth, change and fullness of life. In this sense, Rossetti's words are a kind of analogue of Christ's words, 'Whosoever shall seek to save his life shall lose it; and whosoever shall lose his life shall preserve it.' Perhaps, death on these terms is better than birth; it is certainly the necessary condition of new birth.

The second challenge in her words comes to our (post-) modern religious sensibilities about death, judgement and the New Creation. When Rossetti says that 'Death is better far than birth' she speaks into a context where belief in the New Jerusalem and God's ultimate judgement at the Second Coming of Christ might be held with relative respectability. It is not so clear that such a position might now be held without some embarrassment. Rossetti invites those of us of faith to both interrogate what we believe about the coming of the Kingdom, and participate in it. It is one of the abiding challenges and opportunities of Advent. In this chastened, unenforcing era of faith,[17] it would be absurd to require Christians dogmatically to adhere to classic doctrines. However, each of us is surely wise to reflect on where we stand regarding them and ask what it may yet be possible to believe.

Day Thirteen

The Chiefest Among Ten Thousand

When sick of life and all the world,
How sick of all the earth but Thee,
I lift mine eyes up to the hills,
Eyes of my heart that truly see:
I see beyond all death and ills
Refreshing green for heart and eyes;
The golden streets and gateways pearled,
The living trees of paradise.

Oh that a dove's white wings I had
To flee away from this distress
For Thou art in the wilderness
Drawing and leading Thine Own love:
Wherefore it blossoms like a rose,
The solitary place is glad;
There sounds the soft voice of the dove
And there the spicy south wind blows.

Draw us, we will run after Thee;
Call us by name, the name we know;
Call her beloved who was not so,
Beulah and blessed Hepzibah:
That where Thou art I too may be
Bride of the Bridegroom heart to heart;
Thou God, my Love, the Fairest art
Where all things fair and lovely are.

From north and south from east and west
Thy sons and daughters all shall flock
Who built their house upon the Rock
And eagle-like renew their strength:
How glad and glorious is their rest
Whom Thou hast purged from fleshly scum,—
The long-desired is come at length,
The fulness of the time is come.

Then the new heavens and earth shall be
Where righteousness shall dwell indeed:
There shall be no more blight nor need
Nor barrier of the tossing sea;
No sun and moon alternating
For God shall be the Light thereof,
No sorrow more no death no sting
For God shall reign and God is Love.

As so often with Rossetti, this poem is in deep and dynamic relationship with the language of the Bible. Indeed, this unpublished version shares an opening verse with a poem included in *Verses* called 'I Will Lift Up Mine Eyes to the Hills'. Both poems make Psalm 121 a key conversation partner. It is one of the great psalms of protection and hope, a song that is made to be sung or said, and that fills one's heart with wonder.[18] 'I will lift up mine eyes to the hills, from whence cometh my help,' the psalmist sings, acknowledging that it is from the heights that God's grace comes; from the heights that s/he will be lifted from the depths.

In 'The Chiefest', Rossetti directly addresses the 'sickness unto death' at the heart of human being, a sickness that can overwhelm us, and arguably threatened to overwhelm her at various points in her life. She counterpoints this deep human drive with a determination to lift up the 'eyes of [her] heart' to see beyond all forms of death to the 'living trees of paradise'. Her images of 'golden streets' and 'living trees' draw on the poetry of St John's vision in the Apocalypse. The reader is invited into an eschatological vision that takes us beyond the passing beauties and wonders of this world to find that more permanent vision of glory. To enter this eschatological time and space requires commitment and desire, allied to will.

Just as we orientate ourselves to the eschatological vision, Rossetti pushes in another direction: into the wilderness with Christ. The speaker longs for the 'dove's white wings' – those that descended on Christ and anointed him as God's son – for thereby she might be where Christ is:

> For Thou art in the wilderness
> Drawing and leading Thine Own love:
> Wherefore it blossoms like a rose,
> The solitary place is glad;

As Christians, we may be filled at this time of year with longing for Isaiah-like visions of fulfilment – of the dry places blossoming – yet we are called to wrestle with a God who dwells in the wilderness. This is the God who knows, in Christ, its temptations, but also its ironic riches. There is, as contemporary writer Belden C. Lane puts it, 'solace in fierce landscapes'.[19] This applies even – perhaps especially – in our ultra-connected, online world where there remains a depth of wonder waiting to be found in the 'solitary place'. Perhaps, Advent – like Lent – offers an opportunity for us to find 'gladness' in retreat and wilderness. Rare flowers blossom there, along with the risks presented by wild animals. In the wilderness, we may be exposed to terror and truth.

In Isaiah 62, the prophet writes, 'Thou shalt no more be termed Forsaken; neither shall thy land any more be termed Desolate: but thou shalt be called Hephzibah, and thy land Beulah: for the LORD delighteth in thee, and thy land shall be married.' Rossetti's parsing of this verse in her poem reminds us that 'Hephzibah' means 'my delight is in you', while 'Beulah' means 'married'. Rossetti deploys the Advent language of 'bride' and 'bridegroom' in personal terms:

That where Thou art I too may be
Bride of the Bridegroom heart to heart;

However, this language is the meeting-point of the personal
and the corporate. The union of love is the vocation of the
faithful community, called into delight and 'marriage' in the
divine vision:

From north and south from east and west
Thy sons and daughters all shall flock
Who built their house upon the Rock
And eagle-like renew their strength ...

Then the new heavens and earth shall be
Where righteousness shall dwell indeed:
There shall be no more blight nor need
Nor barrier of the tossing sea;
No sun and moon alternating
For God shall be the Light thereof,
No sorrow more no death no sting
For God shall reign and God is Love.

This is a *tour de force*. Rossetti brings together not only the
personal and the corporate, but a kind of poetic midrash on
the Bible: herein lies a vision that stretches in five stanzas from
one person negotiating mortality and looking out on the hills
through to a properly apocalyptic vision of God's eternal reign
of love. It is mystical and yet earthy; it is visionary and yet
grounded. It is heaven stooped to earth. It anticipates that
which draws ever nearer in this Advent season: Christ's coming
to us as one of us, calling us away from sin into the fullness of
life.

Day Fourteen

When My Heart is Vexed, I Will Complain

'O Lord, how canst Thou say Thou lovest me?
　Me whom Thou settest in a barren land,
　Hungry and thirsty on the burning sand,
Hungry and thirsty where no waters be
Nor shadows of date-bearing tree:—
O Lord, how canst Thou say Thou lovest me?'

'I came from Edom by as parched a track,
　As rough a track beneath My bleeding feet.
　I came from Edom seeking thee, and sweet
I counted bitterness; I turned not back
But counted life as death, and trod
The winepress all alone: and I am God.'

'Yet, Lord, how canst Thou say Thou lovest me?
　For Thou art strong to comfort: and could I
　But comfort one I love, who, like to die,
Lifts feeble hands and eyes that fail to see
In one last prayer for comfort—nay,
I could not stand aside or turn away.'

'Alas! thou knowest that for thee I died
　For thee I thirsted with the dying thirst;
　I, Blessed, for thy sake was counted cursed,
In sight of men and angels crucified:
All this and more I bore to prove
My love, and wilt thou yet mistrust My love?'

'Lord, I am fain to think Thou lovest me,
    For Thou art all in all and I am Thine;
    And lo! Thy love is better than new wine,
And I am sick of love in loving Thee.
    But dost Thou love me? speak and save,
For jealousy is cruel as the grave.'

'Nay, if thy love is not an empty breath
    My love is as thine own—deep answers deep.
    Peace, peace: I give to my beloved sleep,
Not death but sleep, for love is strong as death:
    Take patience; sweet thy sleep shall be,
Yea, thou shalt wake in Paradise with Me.'

In Proverbs 13.12, the writer says, 'Hope deferred maketh the heart sick: but *when* the desire cometh, *it is* a tree of life' (my italics). The theme of 'hope deferred' returns again and again in Rossetti's work. Her poetry – like the Christian life itself – is held in tension between the 'not-yet' and the riches of 'yet-to-come'. Human being is caught between the dream of completion and satisfaction and the facts of self-destruction. Hope is present in the promises of Christ, yet in our waiting we so often fall into a kind of 'sickness'. When the true fulfilment and shape of our calling is found, it is a 'tree of life'. Christ, for Christians, is – of course – the Tree of Life itself.

If Christ is to be the true Tree of Life, that tree must be located in the facts of a life. One of the things I adore in this poem is its psalm-like honesty. Its very title, 'When My Heart is Vexed, I Will Complain', is a manifesto dedicated to utter truth. Its typically nineteenth-century wording – the word 'vex' has rather fallen out of fashion today – disguises the rage and frustration held within it. If the title were to be translated into contemporary English it's hard to deny it would contain some pretty fruity expletives. In a nineteenth-century context, where middle-class Christian women would have been expected to show virtues of self-abnegation, forbearance and modesty (at least in public), this poem sears in its honest wrestling with hope-deferred and hope-known.

The speaker – who may be Christ, who may profoundly identify with Christ – wrestles with and explores a series of biblical images, at once familiar and disturbing. Lines two and three of each stanza form a series of striking couplets that challenge the reader with their honesty: 'Me whom Thou settest in a barren land, / Hungry and thirsty on the burning sand', 'For thee I thirsted with the dying thirst; / I, Blessed, for thy sake was counted cursed', and so on. All of this is framed in a context where the speaker asks, 'O Lord, how canst Thou say Thou lovest me?' Rossetti's handling of that plaintive question keeps, I think, just the right side of the melodramatic. What holds its cry of doubt, pain and bewilderment in place is her use of those familiar biblical tropes already mentioned.

'O Lord, how canst Thou say Thou lovest me?' Perhaps one has to have had certain experiences – of pain, hate, exclusion, for example – to properly take hold of what this question gestures towards. As I read it, I am reminded again of the opening to Martin Scorsese's adaptation of Kanzantzakis's *The Last Temptation of Christ*. We witness Christ stumbling through the wilderness clutching at his head and face in a demented manner. The voice-over (in Jesus' voice) says, 'God loves me, I know he loves me. I wish he'd stop.' If its register is slightly different from Rossetti's, both lines gesture towards similar problems: the strangeness of God's love. We might want 'love' to have the character of comfort, a kind of abundance of good feelings and gesture; however, God's economy often has a different character. The love embedded in the facts of the universe is not soppy or safe. So often it pushes us out into barren lands and bleak terrain. We may say, with Rossetti's speaker, 'Thy love is better than new wine, / And I am sick of love in loving Thee.' However, that love – true, unquenchable, consistent – may lead towards those famous words in Psalm 22: 'My strength is dried up like a potsherd; and my tongue cleaveth to my jaws; and thou hast brought me into the dust of death.' And we might find in them the character of grace.

The Third Week of Advent

'Enough for Him ...'

Advent Three

Advent (1885)

Sooner or later: yet at last
The Jordan must be past;

It may be he will overflow
His banks the day we go;

It may be that his cloven deep
Will stand up on a heap.

Sooner or later: yet one day
We all must pass that way;

Each man, each woman, humbled, pale,
Pass veiled within the veil;

Child, parent, bride, companion,
Alone, alone, alone.

For none a ransom can be paid,
A suretyship be made:

I, bent by mine own burden, must
Enter my house of dust;

I, rated to the full amount,
Must render mine account.

When earth and sea shall empty all
Their graves of great and small;

When earth wrapped in a fiery flood
Shall no more hide her blood;

When mysteries shall be revealed;
All secrets be unsealed;

When things of night, when things of shame,
Shall find at last a name,

Pealed for a hissing and a curse
Throughout the universe:

Then, Awful Judge, most Awful God,
Then cause to bud Thy rod,

To bloom with blossoms, and to give
Almonds; yea, bid us live.

I please Thyself with Thee, I plead
Thee in our utter need:

Jesus, most Merciful of Men,
Show mercy on us then;

Lord God of Mercy and of men,
Show mercy on us then.

In Jewish and Christian thought, the Jordan exercises considerable metaphoric and literal power. It is in the Jordan that John offers a baptism for repentance. It is at the hands of John that Jesus receives baptism and is revealed as God's son. To this day, many Christians find power in visiting that holy site, and flasks of Jordan water are collected and brought back home for use in baptism. Equally, it is reputed to be the place the Israelites crossed to reach the Promised Land. In gospel songs and poetry, the concept of 'crossing the Jordan' acts as an alternative phrase for entering the Kingdom, reaching the Promised Land or reaching heaven.

In this poem,[20] Rossetti meditates on the unavoidability of crossing the Jordan:

Sooner or later: yet one day
We all must pass that way;

Each man, each woman, humbled, pale,
Pass veiled within the veil;

The last phrase is striking. 'Within the veil' is a term used in a variety of places in the Bible, but – in terms of its application to the present poem – most notably in the letter to the Hebrews. In Hebrews 6.19, the writer says, 'which hope we have as an anchor of the soul, both sure and stedfast, and which entereth into that within the veil'. The hope is clearly to be found in Jesus Christ, for, as the next verse states, 'Whither the fore-runner is for us entered, even Jesus, made an high priest for ever after the order of Melchisedec.' In Hebrews, the one who enters into the sanctuary of God is Christ; Christ takes on the being of the priest in the old Temple, who entered the presence of God within the veil. However, Christ is revealed as that priest for all time. Rossetti indicates that none of us can avoid making that passage for ourselves. We enter humbled, pale, to face judgement. 'Child, parent, bride, companion' – no matter our place or role – we enter 'alone, alone, alone'. This thrice-repeated 'alone' only underlines the 'aloneness' of the human journey.

Having established the universal fact of death and the unavoidability that each must cross the river to the eternal, Rossetti brings the poem into the first-person:

I, bent by mine own burden, must
Enter my house of dust;

I, rated to the full amount,
Must render mine account.

There is something disconcerting about the phrase 'house of dust' here. Houses should be places of shelter and safety; places with the potential to become homes. Yet this dwelling-place is only dust; it might then be a metaphor for the body itself, made from dust and to dust it shall return.

Having made this poem of judgement and journey and King-dom 'personal', Rossetti closes the poem in extraordinarily lyrical mode, with the repeated use of 'When' building a mood of momentum and expectation. This is poetry in anticipatory mode. One might almost hear her repeating a rhetorical 'And on that day...' It is eschatological, and rhetorically beautiful. It anticipates the Judgement that is coming towards us rather than us travelling towards it. Of course, as so often with Rossetti, there is tension here: we must live our lives in what might be called a 'diachronic' manner – that is, sequenced through time. But God's Kingdom, as Rossetti acknowledges, comes to meet us and is unavoidable: when 'mysteries shall be revealed ...'; 'When things of night, when things of shame / Shall find at last a name ...'

As participants in God's reality, time and truth, Christians – theologically at least – *know* judgement is coming; this is one of the central cadences of Advent. Knowing this, we can ask God for his grace. It is one of the possibilities of inter-cession. In the closing section, Rossetti takes us away again from the individual back to the corporate; from 'I' to 'we'. God is 'awful' – simultaneously terrifying and full of awe. God is judge. However, as the poem draws to its close, Rossetti finally blends 'I' and 'we'. Corporately and individually, we may be under judgement, but – in the closing lines – her speaker comes back to the Temple sanctuary, where Christ is high priest. She implores him for mercy in the face and fact of judgement. The biblical Greek for veil is *katapetasma*. It has implications of covering or a spreading over. Here we are arguably taken to strange paradoxes of Christ – both priest and sacrifice/victim, the one who covers us with mercy and grace and yet receives our violence. Rossetti's speaker – like any one of us might – knows the inescapable fact of death and judgement and yet, 'within the veil', asks Christ to provide an abundance of mercy and grace.

Day Sixteen

De Profundis

Oh why is heaven built so far,
   Oh why is earth set so remote?
I cannot reach the nearest star
   That hangs afloat.

I would not care to reach the moon,
   One round monotonous of change;
Yet even she repeats her tune
   Beyond my range.

I never watch the scattered fire
   Of stars, or sun's far-trailing train,
But all my heart is one desire,
   And all in vain:

For I am bound with fleshly bands,
   Joy, beauty, lie beyond my scope;
I strain my heart, I stretch my hands,
   And catch at hope.

It would be absurd to claim that Christina Rossetti and Oscar
Wilde belonged to anything other than different milieux. If
both were Victorians, Rossetti's formation was mid-century,
while Wilde became a central figure of the *fin de siècle*; Rossetti
was a Christian, whereas Wilde found no great comfort in
God. However, both wrote pieces titled 'de profundis' or 'out
of the depths'. For Wilde, it took the form of his famous letter
to Bosie from Reading Gaol. In it he explores, with rigour and

emotion, the hedonism of his youth and his present sufferings. He examines his growing identification with Christ in prison. In the letter, he claims, 'Christ's place indeed is with the poets.'

If Wilde's vision is Romantic – viewing Christ as an individualist artist; in short, like Wilde himself – Rossetti's cry from out of the depths seeks to offer a conscious echo of the psalms, specifically Psalm 130. In this psalm, another of the Song of Ascents – which, depending on which authorities one trusts, were sung either by the people as they ascended the road to Jerusalem on pilgrimage, or by the priests as they ascended the steps to minister in the Temple – the sense of longing is profound: 'Out of the depths have I cried unto thee, O Lord. / Lord, hear my voice: let thine ears be attentive to the voice of my supplications.'

In Rossetti's poem the sense of distance between earth and heaven, person and God, the depths and the heights, is profound and can almost not be scoped or spanned. The longing in Rossetti's lyric is almost painful:

> Oh why is heaven built so far,
>   Oh why is earth set so remote?
> I cannot reach the nearest star
>   That hangs afloat.

Rossetti presents us with a vision of the 'vault of heaven'. A scientific reading of the universe might find her language absurd, yet such criticism fails to meet the lyric gambit at stake; when Rossetti's speaker suggests she cannot reach the nearest star or (in the next stanza) the moon, what is at issue is a kind of child-like engagement with the wonders of creation. Faith is not childish, but child-like: in Rossetti's language we are back in that childhood realm where we dream of touching the curtain of night, where it can seem that if only one had a ladder one might climb up to the moon. The kingdom of childhood is not to be mocked here; it is a place where – as in poetry and in faith – new worlds of imagination and new possibilities of meaning are forged. In poetry as much as in childhood, time and space and wonder may be folded together to create new imaginative configurations.

Yet there is a sense that the wonders of creation are limited in this poem, as compared to the heights of God. If there is a child-like quality of attention, it is ultimately reserved for the divine. The moon is 'monotonous', completing its monthly cycle; equally, even the 'scattered fire / Of stars' or the 'sun's far-trailing train' have limited power. Whether firing up the blackness of night or blazing in the daytime, these forms of fiery light are secondary to that offered by God. And yet ... the fire of the speaker's desire – her eros – is not to be satisfied:

> But all my heart is one desire,
>   And all in vain:

Why? Because she is 'bound with fleshly bands'. She strains her heart and stretches her hands and reaches for hope. The poem ends without resolution. The tension remains in the text. The image that is conjured is of a body seeking to escape gravity. This is no mere physical gravity, but a spiritual one. This is a desire that knows the glory of the object sought, but knows also the limitations of this life.

One of the questions for people of faith reading this poem is, 'What shall be my primary gravitational pull during this time of Advent?' It is a time when most of us experience multiple pulls on our time, identities and priorities. Such is the contemporary way of Christmas! We find it almost impossible to focus on Advent as a discrete season, and should one attempt to do so with too much gusto one is likely to be seen as priggish or a Scrooge. I'm not quite sure what the solution is. One has to live in the context in which one is set. And yet, I am mesmerized by the image of a body seeking escape velocity from the pressures – commercial, social, cultural – imposed by consumerist conceptions of 'the festive'. Perhaps it is in prayer that we might most readily go into orbit – not around this earth on which we find ourselves set, but around the God in whose presence one catches at hope.

Day Seventeen

Golden Silences

There is silence that saith, 'Ah me!'
  There is silence that nothing saith;
    One the silence of life forlorn,
    One the silence of death;
One is, and the other shall be.

One we know and have known for long,
  One we know not, but we shall know,
    All we who have ever been born;
    Even so, be it so,—
There is silence, despite a song.

Sowing day is a silent day,
  Resting night is a silent night;
    But whoso reaps the ripened corn
    Shall shout in his delight,
While silences vanish away.

The title of this poem gestures towards a hackneyed proverb, 'Silence is golden, speech is silver'. The implication that silence is worth more than speech is predicated, perhaps, on how readily our species loves to gabble and pile up words. Equally, silence has political and cultural horizons, often used to deprive people of agency and identity. Women, LGBT people, people of colour and children all stand among those who have experienced the use of silence as a power technique.

    This poem, included in *A Pageant and Other Poems*, deploys

Rossetti's technical gift for nuance and the oblique to explore silence as a space for identity, meaning and relationship, as much as a place where voices are shut down. 'Golden Silences' acknowledges the multiplicity of silence; it acknowledges that there is mystery and meaning within its many registers. If the opening stanza offers a familiar opposition – between the silence of forlorn life and the silence of death – the poem unfolds subtler riches as it develops.

In stanza two, the speaker reveals that she has known forlorn silence 'for long'. 'Forlorn' is a tasty word, full of implications of loss, abandonment, ruin and even disgrace. Given the title of the poem, its use is intriguing and hints at the mysteries embedded in the notion of silence. Silence may be golden, but that popular hackneyed conception may not be adequate to the facts of a real life – a life held in the balance of loss and abandonment and the ruin of hopes and promise; a life held in the balance of the ultimate silence we shall all face in death. In the light of this analysis, I find the speaker's final line in stanza two, 'There is silence, despite a song', almost unutterably moving. Song may have many registers – from joy to pleasure to doubt and lament – but every mode of life's song is ultimately to be read through silence.

Then, there is this extraordinary closing stanza:

Sowing day is a silent day,
   Resting night is a silent night;
      But whoso reaps the ripened corn
   Shall shout in his delight,
While silences vanish away.

Having articulated the power of silence, the speaker develops her theme in terms of metaphors of sowing and harvest. These images are simultaneously biblical and secular; they gesture towards the facts of life understood in both natural and revelatory terms. Silence is pervasive – in the new day and at night. Yet, the speaker claims that whoever reaps the fruits of silence shall 'shout in his delight, / While silences vanish away.'

Ultimately – in the hands of God? – even the silences generated by death and loss shall flee away.

One is reminded here of the seventeenth-century French carol 'Venez Divin Messie/O Come, Divine Messiah', with words by Abbé Simon Pellegrin:

O come, divine Messiah!
The world in silence waits the day
When hope shall sing its triumph,
And sadness flee away.

Silence, as any sensitive person can recognize, has many tenors and moments. People of faith are likely to count themselves among those who wish to cultivate silence as a place to encounter the holy, even when that proves a profound challenge. Silence is dangerous because of what it may expose in ourselves and others. It has the power of revelation embedded within it. It is also dangerous as a technique for the control of others. However, I sense that a life lived without acknowledging silence's glories and terrors is not quite a life lived faithfully. It is less than abundant life, even when silence is experienced as forlorn. Rossetti's poem is honest about the nature of silence; when one reads it during a time of preparation for Christmas it challenges too. It dares us to stick with silence – God's, our own, others' – in the hope of receiving the joyous harvest in the Christ-Child on Christmas Day.

Day Eighteen

Of Him That Was Ready To Perish

Lord, I am waiting, weeping, watching for Thee:
My youth and hope lie by me buried and dead,
My wandering love hath not where to lay its head
Except Thou say 'Come to Me.'

My noon is ended, abolished from life and light,
My noon is ended, ended and done away,
My sun went down in the hours that still were day,
And my lingering day is night.

How long, O Lord, how long in my desperate pain
Shall I weep and watch, shall I weep and long for Thee?
Is Thy grace ended, Thy love cut off from me?
How long shall I long in vain?

O God Who before the beginning hast seen the end,
Who hast made me flesh and blood, not frost and not fire,
Who hast filled me full of needs and love and desire
And a heart that craves a friend,

Who hast said 'Come to Me and I will give thee rest,'
Who hast said 'Take on thee My yoke and learn of Me,'
Who calledst a little child to come to Thee,
And pillowedst John on Thy breast;

Who spak'st to women that followed Thee sorrowing,
Bidding them weep for themselves and weep for their own;
Who didst welcome the outlaw adoring Thee all alone,
And plight Thy word as a King,—

By Thy love of these and of all that ever shall be,
    By Thy love of these and of all the born and unborn,
    Turn Thy gracious eyes on me and think no scorn
        Of me, not even of me.

Beside Thy Cross I hang on my cross in shame,
    My wounds, weakness, extremity cry to Thee:
    Bid me also to Paradise, also me
        For the glory of Thy Name.

'My noon is ended'. It is an evocative phrase. Noon, when the sun should be highest in the sky; noon, suggestive of a life at its fullest reach and blossoming. In the poetry of the great Emily Dickinson, God is sometimes designated as 'the man of noon'. It is, for Dickinson, not necessarily a positive connection, gesturing towards an over-mastering conception of the divine.

In 'Of Him That Was Ready To Perish', 'my noon is ended' gestures, of course, to life beyond its zenith. However, given its context – Christ on the cross – it has other implications too. When the speaker says, 'My sun went down in the hours that still were day', there is a gesture towards solidarity with Christ on the cross: for, as the Gospel records indicate, in the hour of his suffering the sun was covered over. This poem, then, is a poem of experience, written in the full knowledge of what life is like beyond the beginnings. If life can be costly and troubling at any age, a mature life brings its own nuances, especially the mature life of faith. When I think of my own faith journey – one marked by a powerful conversion experience in my twenties – it's fascinating to consider how it's changed. The 'noon' of conversion – its intensity, its freshness and sharpness – has been eclipsed; yet there is greater depth in the shadows. In middle age, faith is rarely scintillating, but even in the dryness and longing there is greater reality.

Perhaps most of us, middle aged or not, lack the sharpness of tears that Rossetti indicates here. Perhaps few of us know what it is to ask, 'How long shall I long in vain?' And yet ... in the hard work of seeking to be faithful in prayer and praise,

I, along with so many others, know that cry, 'How long, O Lord?' I feel it most sharply in intercession, during times when the world seems to be spinning off its axis. Ours is a world that so often seems caught between hope and suffering; between glimpses of glory and humanity's sinful capacity to debase creation and ourselves. Our longing is cast, as Rossetti suggests, into a crucible of God's eternity. In this crucible, God's omniscience is balanced by his self-emptying into Jesus Christ. This is a God who 'before the beginning hast seen the end,' yet is caught up in the particularities of our world:

> Who hast made me flesh and blood, not frost and not fire,
> Who hast filled me full of needs and love and desire
> And a heart that craves a friend,

This God is no coldly distant maker, but flesh and blood like us. The following stanzas ache with simple beauty, as they catalogue Christ's humanity:

> Who hast said 'Come to Me and I will give thee rest,'
> Who hast said 'Take on thee My yoke and learn of Me,'
> Who calledst a little child to come to Thee,
> And pillowedst John on Thy breast;

> Who spak'st to women that followed Thee sorrowing,
> Bidding them weep for themselves and weep for their own;
> Who didst welcome the outlaw adoring Thee all alone,
> And plight Thy word as a King,—

Even a middle-aged, cynical priest like me, tumbling ever further away from the noon of life and the first wonder of conversion, cannot deny the flowing, lyrical tenderness of these lines. They are beguiling and moving. As the poem closes, Rossetti draws us back towards the cross at noon, rather than Dickinson's mighty 'Man of Noon'. In these lines, her speaker knows how longing meets personal need in honest self-examination. She asks that Christ's grace and tenderness be available to the one who wishes to take up her cross and follow the Living God. This concern to follow the way of Christ is as pungent in the season of Advent as in any other:

> By Thy love of these and of all that ever shall be,
>   By Thy love of these and of all the born and unborn,
>   Turn Thy gracious eyes on me and think no scorn
>   Of me, not even of me.

> Beside Thy Cross I hang on my cross in shame,
>   My wounds, weakness, extremity cry to Thee:
>   Bid me also to Paradise, also me
>   For the glory of Thy Name.

Day Nineteen

'He Cannot Deny Himself'

Love still is Love, and doeth all things well,
Whether He shows me heaven or hell
   Or earth in her decay
   Passing away
   On a day.

Love still is Love, tho' He should say, 'Depart.'
And break my incorrigible heart,
   And set me out of sight
   Widowed of light
   In the night.

Love still is Love, is Love, if He should say,
'Come,' on that uttermost dread day;
   'Come,' unto very me,
   'Come where I be,
   Come and see.'

Love still is Love, whatever comes to pass:
O Only Love, make me Thy glass,
   Thy pleasure to fulfil
   By loving still
   Come what will.

Understanding the varieties and simplicities of love is not
something – in my view – for which the contemporary world
displays a genius. Ours is a time where love is too readily
resolved into romance and/or sex. In and of itself, I don't see a

problem with the joyous, emptying possibilities of sex or even the slightly silly fripperies of romance. Sex, in particular, is one of those aspects of life that can draw us – along with death and religion – to a deeper understanding of the drives of our bewildering lives. Equally, few of us would wish to abandon the possibilities of romance, understood in its proper order. However, to have an excessive and irrational commitment to 'romance' or 'sex' strikes me as almost to guarantee a mis-understanding of love.

'He Cannot Deny Himself' presents a fascinating and ulti-mately challenging meditation on the riches and possibilities of love. Its stanzas return, again and again, to the same line – 'Love still is Love' – giving it both the character of a child's rhyme and the feel of an axiomatic argument. However, it is a reminder that in the hands of a skilled poet, repetition is always 'non-identical'; it shifts and moves us into new places, even as it offers us the same structure. Indeed, this poem deploys another classic Rossettian technique, *anaphora* – that is, the repetition of a certain word or phrase at the beginning of successive lines of writing. In the third stanza, the repeated use of the word 'come' draws the reader deeper into the text. In this way, poetic repetition shares similarities with liturgical repetition. We may repeat a series of lines, a litany, and yet each subtly alters us and invites us into new space and time. 'He Cannot Deny Himself' offers a litany of love's riches and possibilities.

The title of the poem is itself fascinating. In a contemporary Advent context, one might take it as a signal of lack of self-control. In an age of gin, whisky and cheese Advent calendars, an inability to 'deny oneself' conjures images of someone who has ripped open every 'window' on the calendar on the first day of December and now sits in a stupor of cheese and gin. Our consumer culture almost seems to require us to 'give in' and let ourselves have little treats; we go shopping or sit online looking at shoes and handbags or tweed jackets and tell our-selves we cannot deny ourselves and our friends say, 'Well, you deserve it.' The ironies of Rossetti's poem lie in a presentation of love as 'self-giving', as abundant availability and grace. This is desire that is not self-serving, but self-offering to the other.

I am, as so often, moved by Rossetti's juxtapositions. If this poem's refrain might be accused of sentimentality and banality, even Christmas-card verse, what it gestures towards is not. The poetry lies, perhaps, in the dynamics between the surface simplicity of the words and their metaphysical possibilities. For, when the speaker says 'Love still is Love', it rapidly becomes clear that we are not in a greeting-card world, but one with cost and calling. He who cannot deny himself is faithful in love, 'Whether He shows me heaven or hell'; love still is love, even when Christ breaks 'my incorrigible heart' or invites one into his presence on 'that uttermost dread day'.

In short, 'Love still is Love, whatever comes to pass'. How many of us dare utter that line with sincerity? As I write, I am reminded of the 'Methodist Covenant Prayer' that I encountered in my twenties when, during a period of testing my vocation to holy orders, I was required to worship in a Methodist church. For those of you who are unaware, the 'Covenant Prayer' is prayed corporately during the Covenant Service, which usually takes place around New Year, sometimes on New Year's Eve itself. It invites a shattering commitment to be where God calls us to be:

I am no longer my own, but thine.
Put me to what thou wilt, rank me with whom thou wilt.
Put me to doing, put me to suffering.
Let me be employed for thee or laid aside for thee,
exalted for thee or brought low for thee.
Let me be full, let me be empty.
Let me have all things, let me have nothing.
I freely and heartily yield all things to thy pleasure and
     disposal.
And now, O glorious and blessed God, Father, Son and
     Holy Spirit,
thou art mine, and I am thine.
So be it.

And the covenant which I have made on earth,
let it be ratified in heaven.
Amen.

Whenever I have encountered this prayer, I have asked myself if I dare pray it.

In times of illness, strain and, well, just sheer rubbishness, I have often found it almost impossible to say, with Rossetti, 'Love still is Love, whatever comes to pass'. And yet ... and yet ... Rossetti's line captures one of the profoundest calls of our faith. Our God does not promise an easy ride; our God only promises to be with us till the end of the age. Our God's self-offering of love is not sentimental, easy or cheap. It is the profoundest desire for our flourishing and growth into the likeness of Christ. It is the self-offering of the one in whom, if only we dare meet them, we shall find our deepest, richest selves.

Day Twenty

Lay Up For Yourselves Treasures in Heaven

Treasure plies a feather,
  Pleasure spreadeth wings,
  Taking flight together,—
  Ah! my cherished things.

Fly away, poor pleasure,
  That art so brief a thing:
Fly away, poor treasure,
  That hast so swift a wing.

Pleasure, to be pleasure,
  Must come without a wing;
Treasure, to be treasure,
  Must be a stable thing.

Treasure without feather,
  Pleasure without wings,
Elsewhere dwell together
  And are heavenly things.

One of the peculiar challenges of Christianity is that it keeps two seasons of fasting and repentance. Keeping one season of fasting is demanding enough; to have to keep two might strike some as verging on the absurd. Of course, in the popular mind, there is only one season of fasting: Lent. Advent has become so overwhelmed by Christmas 'brought forward' ever earlier into December it does not register as a season of prayerful restraint. Even our Advent calendars – which can be helpful ways of focusing and waiting – have become marked by indulgence, offering us a foretaste of secular ideas of Christmas feasting. Yet, the simple fact that, liturgically at least, there are two Christian fast seasons should alert even its casual acquaintances to the rigour Christianity holds within it.

I issue this *aide-mémoire* regarding our faith's twin seasons of fasting because the phrase 'Lay up for yourselves treasures in heaven' is likely to be associated with the beginning of Lent, Ash Wednesday, rather than Advent. It is included as one of the Church of England's *Common Worship* scriptural choices for that day and I, like many priests, have used that line as a springboard to preach sermons on possessions and attachments. On Ash Wednesday, the theme of 'where your treasure is, there your heart is also', is ever close to the surface. Of course, during Advent – as one experiences the pressures to consume and indulge ahead of Christmas – this line of Scripture bears equal if not greater weight.

Rossetti frames this poem in terms of Scripture and then does something unexpected. She explores the concept of treasure in terms of flight and feathers; she suggests that so much of what we might consider treasure is pleasure and that such a thing is 'flighty' and weightless. It is – as so often with Rossetti – an ironic move. In popular terms, 'treasure' is associated with gold, jewels and gems piled high. One might place them in a huge chest or a chamber (with, if one is a fan of Tolkien, a dragon on guard). Such treasure is weighty, this-worldly and tangible. It is about as 'this-worldly' and material as a thing can be. And, yet, ironically, for the speaker 'cherished things' are presented as winged and occupied and busily pursuing feathers.

Rossetti's speaker is discreet regarding what might count as her cherished things – yet these almost weightless things ('poor pleasure', 'poor treasure') she invites to fly away and depart. Perhaps like birds' bones these cherished things have the appearance of solidity, but are hollow. Perhaps their hollowness is what makes them capable of flight. Intriguingly, it is not pleasure or treasure itself that she disavows. There is no pious disavowal of pleasure as essentially sinful in this poem. Rather, the puzzle she presents is to suggest that flighty pleasure isn't true pleasure at all:

> Pleasure, to be pleasure,
>   Must come without a wing;
> Treasure, to be treasure,
>   Must be a stable thing.

Rather than formulate an argument, she draws us deeper into a participative mystery. Her suggestion is that true riches are wingless and stable. However, if the early part of this poem is ironic, the claims about the nature of true riches are presented without archness. The stability on offer is not that of base materiality, but the consistent character found in God and heaven:

> Treasure without feather,
>   Pleasure without wings,
> Elsewhere dwell together
>   And are heavenly things.

We are perhaps too inclined to see 'heaven' as other-worldly; as the very acme of 'flighty' and the immaterial. In this poem, Rossetti reverses the polarities. In her speaker's economy – which aligns itself with God's economy, of course – 'heaven' is presented as the most material, grounded and solid of things. It is present and available, as George Herbert presents it so elegantly in 'Prayer (I)' as 'in ordinary'. The extraordinary challenge for us – as much as for Rossetti or Herbert – is to draw closer to the material solidity of the true treasures of heaven. As we draw ever closer to Christmas, perhaps it is time once again to redraw our spiritual scope. What is the true treasure? What are our cherished things that create the illusions of solidity, but are weightless and fly away even as we grasp after them? What, in the end, are our 'cherished things' and do they have the lasting character of heaven?

Day Twenty-One

Winter: My Secret

I tell my secret? No indeed, not I:
Perhaps some day, who knows?
But not today; it froze, and blows, and snows,
And you're too curious: fie!
You want to hear it? well:
Only, my secret's mine, and I won't tell.

Or, after all, perhaps there's none:
Suppose there is no secret after all,
But only just my fun.
Today's a nipping day, a biting day;
In which one wants a shawl,
A veil, a cloak, and other wraps:
I cannot ope to every one who taps,
And let the draughts come whistling thro' my hall;
Come bounding and surrounding me,
Come buffeting, astounding me,
Nipping and clipping thro' my wraps and all.
I wear my mask for warmth: who ever shows
His nose to Russian snows
To be pecked at by every wind that blows?
You would not peck? I thank you for good will,
Believe, but leave that truth untested still.

Spring's an expansive time: yet I don't trust
March with its peck of dust,
Nor April with its rainbow-crowned brief showers,

Nor even May, whose flowers
One frost may wither thro' the sunless hours.

Perhaps some languid summer day,
When drowsy birds sing less and less,
And golden fruit is ripening to excess,
If there's not too much sun nor too much cloud,
And the warm wind is neither still nor loud,
Perhaps my secret I may say,
Or you may guess.

Rossetti's avowedly secular poem 'Winter: My Secret' has been taken as significant for her whole poetic oeuvre and has been a centrepiece for many critical works on her poetics. If it is not devotional and, therefore, arguably not of central interest in an Advent/Christmas book, it earns its keep not only in the way it engages with the wintry themes of this season, but in its capacity to tease and intrigue: key Rossettian themes. It invites its readers, both secular and religious, to play and question. Most of all, it invites its readers into elusiveness and mystery.

Constance Hassett has suggested that 'Winter: My Secret' indicates '[Rossetti's] interest in enigmatic exchanges and verbal evasion'.[21] It negotiates secrecy and reserve while being flirtatious with the edges of taboo. If, in her devotional verse, she seriously engaged with the poetry and theology of reserve developed by theologians like Keble, this poem shows her exploring reserve in a secular context. Hassett suggests that 'Winter: My Secret' 'considers the wonderfully paradoxical possibilities of flagrant concealment and garrulous reticence'.[22] Rossetti constructs a series of 'teases' in the poem:

I tell my secret? No, indeed, not I
...
Suppose there is no secret after all
...
Perhaps my secret I may say,
Or you may guess.

The secret could be many things – the writer's 'winter', her frigidity or virginity or the 'golden fruit' of fulfilment. It may be the writer's subjectivity, locked in by the 'I' that is performed at both the beginning and the end of the opening line. As the poem later claims, 'I wear my mask for warmth'. The speaker in the poem also wears 'a veil, a cloak, and other wraps'. Rossetti's speaker is, then, allusive, elusive and fundamentally doubled – a mask wearer whose 'secret' seems to be structurally locked up. As Hassett helpfully summarizes, 'Winter: My Secret' 'manages to be simultaneously flagrant and reserved, to withhold a secret even as it enfolds the hope of a poetry that is sensuous, expansive and self-revealing.'[23] Its work of masking creates doubled effects, which raises questions about the poet's identity and generates mysterious effects.

The concept of 'mask' is an icon of both concealment and revelation. Masks cover up, but they can also show forth: our choice of mask can tell a great deal about us. Academics have explored how the concept speaks powerfully into the wider attempts of nineteenth-century middle-class women poets to articulate a tradition of poetry in the shadow of and beyond the binds of patriarchy. In the poetics of an earlier generation of women poets like Anna-Laeticia Barbauld, 'winter' was coded as 'sublime'. In her poem 'Inscription for an Ice-House', winter is seen as masculine, over-mastering and excessive. It arguably models how women as poets have to negotiate their exclusion from full, creative subjectivity. In so far as Rossetti herself engages with that discourse around winter in 'Winter: My Secret', she foregrounds a teasing, secretive strategy. She does not use a direct route. It is deliberately elusive.

This book, of course, is not a place to dwell at length on those explorations. Rather, I want to invite further reflection on masking and mystery; I want to reflect on the power, even the necessity, of masks during a season like Advent. This may surprise some readers. It is not unreasonable to code Advent as a season for removing masks and looking face to face with our fellow travellers and pilgrims and to dare to expose our human reality to God. There is much to commend this reading of Advent and, in large measure, I find it persuasive. However, I still think Rossetti's strategic use of masking in 'Winter: My Secret' has significance for our Advent practices. For, just as she deploys teasing, allusive and elusive strategies to negotiate the sublime power of winter, I wonder if the careful use of masks might enable us to live this pressured season.

Rossetti says, 'I wear my mask for warmth'. I so often feel under profound strain during December; the exposure to others' needs and demands can feel eviscerating. By the time Christmas Day comes I feel utterly spent. Perhaps that is a professional risk when one is a priest, but I am sure that others must feel this too. To find a way to survive and thrive, even if it requires wearing a mask, should not be readily dismissed as sinful. It may be what makes living in a time of strain and challenge possible.

The Fourth Week of Advent

'What Can I Give Him?'

Advent Four

Advent (1885/6)

Earth grown old, yet still so green,
  Deep beneath her crust of cold
Nurses fire unfelt, unseen:
  Earth grown old.

We who live are quickly told:
Millions more lie hid between
  Inner swathings of her fold.

When will fire break up her screen?
  When will life burst thro' her mould?
Earth, earth, earth, thy cold is keen,
  Earth grown old.

As we draw close to the wonder and vulnerability of Christmas morning – replete with its images of stars and mangers, stables and a new-born – this poem grants us pause. In our minds, when we think of 'swathing' or 'swaddling' bands we understandably jump immediately towards images drawn from Victorian carols: of the baby Christ in swathing bands. Rossetti's picture of the 'inner swathings' of the earth in 'Advent' is both tougher and richer than the sentiment performed in most carols.

In this vision, 'earth' – as metaphor for both the world and the condition of life – is simultaneously aged and 'still so green'. There is a factual truth to this: when the earth is covered with a crust of ice or snow, beneath may lie grass, still green, waiting to flourish again. However, the word 'green' also holds within it a traditional poetic representation of 'youth'. In 'Advent', Rossetti surely draws on this sense of green, deployed most famously by Shakespeare's Cleopatra when she speaks of 'my salad days when I was green in judgment, cold in blood'. The fire of life is concealed in an aged, tired world and vice versa. The earth on which we live and of which we are formed is always double-edged: it holds the fire of life as well as the remains of 'millions more'. The swathing bands of earth hold the dead and, as Rossetti's speaker wittily riffs on the old term for the 'living' – the quick – we are 'quickly told'.

From this doubleness and metaphorical play, her speaker plunges the reader into the apocalyptic and eschatological. A new layer of implication and possibility is rehearsed and revealed:

> When will fire break up her screen?
>   When will life burst thro' her mould?
> Earth, earth, earth, thy cold is keen,
>   Earth grown old.

Again, we have multiple layers operating simultaneously: in one sense, Rossetti's words might gesture simply towards the fire of the new year or the sun, while the idea of life bursting through might be a reference to spring. However, the context is Advent. The fire presented here is one offered through the lens of God's new creation; the life that waits to 'burst thro' her mould' is one that will disrupt the natural, pre-established patterns of creation.

If this is a vision of God's new Kingdom, it is grounded in the facts of a cold December world that – as becomes clear in the poem that gives this book its title – is shaped by 'frosty wind made moan':

> Earth, earth, earth, thy cold is keen,
>   Earth grown old.

The triple use of 'earth' runs the risk of being too much; yet its incantatory repetition feels melancholic, almost disbelieving. It is as if in the face of the facts of winter's icy realities, it is almost impossible to believe in the possibilities of the Kingdom, of new life, of the dead raised to judgement. And yet, in a time of 'Earth grown old', what else might a person of faith do? We are called by God to believe in God's reality breaking in, and breaking up the established and often oppressive status quo. We are called to do so, even – perhaps especially – when that seems impossible. The people of God are the people of the 'in-between', who say 'soon the new Earth shall come ...' even when the old world still insists otherwise. We are fully aware of the pull of the old world, but we long for the new.

Day Twenty-Three

A Hope Carol

A night was near, a day was near,
  Between a day and night
I heard sweet voices calling clear,
  Calling me:
I heard a whirr of wing on wing,
  But could not see the sight;
I long to see my birds that sing,
  I long to see.

Below the stars, beyond the moon,
  Between the night and day
I heard a rising falling tune
  Calling me:
I long to see the pipes and strings
  Whereon such minstrels play;
I long to see each face that sings,
  I long to see.

Today or may be not today,
  Tonight or not tonight,
All voices that command or pray
  Calling me,
Shall kindle in my soul such fire
  And in my eyes such light
That I shall see that heart's desire
  I long to see.

In my comments on a number of Rossetti's poems, I have sought to explore how she skilfully and intriguingly explores the in-between spaces of identity, faith and the Christian hope; how she invites us to consider that we, as people of faith, exist between the now and the not-yet, this world and the next; how Advent is a time of (forgive the technicality) the 'liminal' or the 'interstitial'. Perhaps this double-sided possibility is no clearer than in the poem 'A Hope Carol'.

Structurally, the poem has a threefold, perhaps even trinitarian, structure. Each eight-line block of the poem uses an abacdbdc rhyming scheme. The rhyme and repetition ensures that the poem moves forward in sections, as well as holding it to a kind of ellipsis. It returns to a kind of longing, again and again; it models a desire for satisfaction and completion that is never quite satisfied. Each time the speaker posits that satisfaction might arrive today or tonight, she questions and defers it. The deferral pushes the hope of satisfaction endlessly into the future, and even at the poem's conclusion there is no satisfaction. Rossetti seems to suggest that in the poetry of hope, longing rather than satisfaction is the constant. Ultimately, the speaker always returns to the refrain, 'I long to see.'

Arguably the imagery she presents is romanticized and reflects the influence of the Pre-Raphaelite movement, with its fascination with the medieval. The poetry is saturated with classic images of birds and stars and moon; the musicians in this poem are 'minstrels' playing pipes and strings. It is hardly an edgy, post-modern scene. However, that doesn't mean that this poem lacks grip and pay-off. At this time of year, most of us are negotiating varieties of romanticized and senti-mentalized festive images. Whether we like it or not, Advent and Christmas have both been colonized by 'olde-worlde' images. For some, the insidious nature of these images make the festive season a write-off, or at best a mere camp display. I see things slightly differently. In a world into which Christianity still wishes to speak, it can come across as priggish and pious to insist that only 'this' way or 'that' counts as proper 'Advent' or 'Christmas'. So-called 'Victorian' or 'kitsch' images of Christmas are part of its discourse and should not be dismissed out of hand.

In such a context, Rossetti's secular carol offers the reader something precisely because of its imagery rather than in spite of it. The 'rising falling tune' is a tune of our culture. It draws us and yet it seems alien. The snow and tinsel of our most sentimentalized Christmas ideas draw us and comfort us and yet we know their limit; they belong to the past and our present, and they satisfy and disappoint in almost equal measure. Rossetti arguably knew that over a century and a half ago. She knows that the place of being human is 'interstitial'; it is shaped by longing and desire, and all the complexities of the in-between. Her poem is secular and religious at the same time; it is present and yet longs for that which is absent; it deals with what has gone and yet desires what is yet to come. Her speaker knows all this and it comes to her as 'fire' – alive, dancing, burning and, perhaps, purifying. This fire calls her – and us – on:

> All voices that command or pray
>   Calling me,
> Shall kindle in my soul such fire
>   And in my eyes such light
> That I shall see that heart's desire
>   I long to see.

Day Twenty-Four (Christmas Eve)

Christmas Eve

Christmas hath darkness
  Brighter than the blazing noon,
Christmas hath a chillness
  Warmer than the heat of June,
Christmas hath a beauty
  Lovelier than the world can show:
For Christmas bringeth Jesus,
  Brought for us so low.

Earth, strike up your music,
  Birds that sing and bells that ring;
Heaven hath answering music
  For all Angels soon to sing:
Earth, put on your whitest
  Bridal robe of spotless snow:
For Christmas bringeth Jesus,
  Brought for us so low.

The seventeenth-century poet Henry Vaughan famously claimed 'there is in God a deep, but dazzling darkness'. It has been taken as a signal by a number of writers, including me, that while God might readily be understood in terms of classic ideas of light and purity, he has an ironic richness. God can be found not only within bright places of glory, but in the dark and shade of life; more than this, that dark is not simply shadowy and lacking, it can be as dazzling as the brightest day.

In her poem for the 'in-between', 'Christmas Eve', Rossetti brings her own sensibility to bear on the dazzling possibilities of God in the dark. Indeed, in the midst of the approach of the Light of the World, she confronts us with quite unexpected irony:

> Christmas hath darkness
>> Brighter than the blazing noon,
> Christmas hath a chillness
>> Warmer than the heat of June

Here she disrupts our assumptions with irony so bold that it verges on the absurd. How can Christmas have darkness brighter than the blazing noon or a 'chillness' warmer than the heat of June? Part of the answer arguably lies in a kind of shock. Rossetti flips our assumptions about the possibilities of Christmas. This is not a cosy time; this is the world turned upside-down. More than that, as we prepare to enter the first moments of Christmas, we find reality disrupted and transformed. God creeps in beside us in the most ironic way possible: not as a king or emperor in a palace, but as a vulnerable peasant's baby. Heat, light, darkness, cold blaze through our ready sentiments. The God who will expose us for what we are, both in the manger and on the Cross, comes into our bewilderment, hope and need.

If there is disruption, there is beauty too. How could there not be? If Jesus comes among us as one who shall expose and bear our sins, he comes as God. God's beauty is part of both his deepest nature and his abiding humility or 'lowliness'. As ever with Rossetti, she brings the sensibility of great visual artists to bear. Just as Rubens and Titian and countless other artists were never afraid to comprehend the incarnation of Christ as a matter unfolding in the plains of Italy or in the towns of Flanders, she brings the Nativity into the December cold of England:

Birds that sing and bells that ring;
Heaven hath answering music
For all Angels soon to sing:
Earth, put on your whitest
Bridal robe of spotless snow:
For Christmas bringeth Jesus,
Brought for us so low.

For some this notion of the 'Bridal robe of spotless snow' might be read as verging on the absurd or ridiculously sentimental (a kind of mid-Victorian Christmas-card scene). I suggest we can approach it rather differently; if the Nativity is a mythic matter (that is, a foundational and theological one rather than a literal matter), we should be ever bold to reimagine it in our context and present. Snow has implications of innocence, but also of risk and cold. It can be dry and terrifying as well as beautiful. Rossetti brings the Nativity into the harsh winters of mid-nineteenth-century England, but she also brings out the sharpness of beauty. The Christ who comes to us in lowliness is full of wonder and beauty, but he comes to us in sharpness of ice and snow; he is exposed and exposing. He delights and he terrifies us too.

If we are deep in snow and wonder as Christmas approaches, we have also travelled far into Rossetti's deceptively simple poetics. 'Christmas Eve' unfolds the Tractarian poetics of 'reserve' in helpful ways. This idea relies on the claim that divine truth is revealed gradually and delightfully, most especially in the tender and discreet deployment of poetry. In 'Christmas Eve', Rossetti is utterly unafraid of simplicity, but she is far from simplistic. Rather, her mature devotional poetics create space for us to participate. Unlike a much earlier poem for Christmas Eve, included below, there is a quiet surety that gives the reader space to breathe. It is not so much that the earlier poem, 'A Christmas Carol', is a failure. It too shows considerable technical skill; rather, it is a little more obvious in its tone (the repeated 'thank Gods' perform an obvious sort of surety and gladness) and betokens a younger, less formed imagination.

A Christmas Carol
(On the Stroke of Midnight) (1849)

Thank God, thank God, we do believe,
Thank God that this is Christmas Eve.
Even as we kneel upon this day,
Even so the ancient legends say
Nearly two thousand years ago
The stalled ox knelt, and even so
The ass knelt full of praise which they
Could not express, while we can pray.
Thank God, thank God, for Christ was born
Ages ago, as on this morn:
In the snow-season undefiled
God came to earth a little Child;
He put His ancient glory by
To live for us, and then to die.

How shall we thank God? how shall we
Thank Him and praise Him worthily?
What will He have Who loved us thus?
What presents will He take from us?
Will He take gold, or precious heap
Of gems, or shall we rather steep
The air with incense, or bring myrrh?
What man will be our messenger
To go to Him and ask His will?
Which having learned we will fulfil
Tho' He choose all we most prefer:—
What man will be our messenger?

Thank God, thank God, the Man is found,
Sure-footed, knowing well the ground.
He knows the road, for this the way
He travelled once, as on this day.
He is our Messenger beside,
He is our Door, and Path, and Guide;
He also is our Offering,

He is the Gift that we must bring.
Let us kneel down with one accord
And render thanks unto the Lord:
For unto us a Child is born
Upon this happy Christmas morn;
For unto us a Son is given,
Firstborn of God and Heir of Heaven.

First Week of Christmas

'If I Were a Shepherd'

Christmas Day

A Christmas Carol
(also known as 'In the Bleak Midwinter') (1872)

In the bleak mid-winter
   Frosty wind made moan,
Earth stood hard as iron,
   Water like a stone;
Snow had fallen, snow on snow,
   Snow on snow,
In the bleak mid-winter
   Long ago.

Our God, Heaven cannot hold Him
   Nor earth sustain;
Heaven and earth shall flee away
   When He comes to reign:
In the bleak mid-winter
   A stable-place sufficed
The Lord God Almighty
   Jesus Christ.

Enough for Him whom cherubim
   Worship night and day,
A breastful of milk
   And a mangerful of hay;
Enough for Him whom angels
   Fall down before,
The ox and ass and camel
   Which adore.

Angels and archangels
　　May have gathered there,
Cherubim and seraphim
　　Thronged the air,
But only His mother
　　In her maiden bliss
Worshipped the Beloved
　　With a kiss.

What can I give Him,
　　Poor as I am?
If I were a shepherd
　　I would bring a lamb,
If I were a wise man
　　I would do my part,—
Yet what I can I give Him,
　　Give my heart.

'A Christmas Carol', also known as 'In the Bleak Midwinter', has become so famous it is almost impossible to make anything but glancing comments about it. It is as ubiquitous as Christmas trees and tinsel, at least within Christian circles. It is a staple of almost every serious Carol Service. I hope, however, that given the imaginative journey we have undertaken this Advent, perhaps we begin to see its treasures anew. At the very least, I hope readers begin to appreciate how 'A Christmas Carol' brings together an abundance of Rossetti's lyrical and theological gifts. In this poem, she displays a lyrical mastery of simultaneous time and space, of the global and particular, of the sweet and the shocking. This is a big poem capable of shaping vast and impressive ideas – 'Heaven cannot hold him' – yet it finds its ultimate dignity in shaping a particular response to God-made-tiny: 'What can I give Him, / Poor as I am?'

Composed for an American magazine, *Scribner's Monthly*, it is almost impossible to read 'A Christmas Carol' without triggering Holst's simple setting *Cranham* as an ear-worm; failing that, Harold Darke's magnificent setting, mostly performed by choirs because of the way it varies the melody from verse to verse, is rarely far away. Yet, 'In the Bleak Midwinter' remains poetry first, and hymn lyrics second. Like all good poetry, its music is found within the words first and the musical settings second. Unlike a song lyric, the poem doesn't need music in order to find its internal song.

Tonally, 'In the Bleak Midwinter' captures a dimension of Christmas that all too often our consumer culture ignores: melancholic evocation. In terms of modern popular music, perhaps the nearest Christmas music comes to capturing this dimension of Christmas is Judy Garland's 'Have Yourself A Merry Little Christmas'. It is tempting to suggest that, because Christmas is so relentlessly cheery and shiny, it creates a shadowy void as its other. I've no doubt about that: our consumerized, secular age concentrates so much pressure on having the best family time at Christmas that it inevitably disappoints. At the same time, I want to suggest the melancholy of Rossetti's poem is found in something more theologically interesting. Her decision to shift the Nativity to a bleak, cold northern winter – about which more in a moment – models a melancholic, frozen environment into which not only may God enter, but it effectively requires it. At a theological level, the physical cold gestures towards the frozen and fixed realities of the human condition in need of God's transformation. Her transposition of the Nativity to a frozen, bleak landscape disrupts any sentimental assumptions one might have about Christ's nativity.

If the opening stanza is scintillating in its construction of a *mise en scène*, it is the second stanza that offers – in eight short lines – an astonishing series of theological gambits:

Our God, Heaven cannot hold Him
   Nor earth sustain;
Heaven and earth shall flee away
   When He comes to reign:
In the bleak mid-winter
   A stable-place sufficed

The Lord God Almighty
Jesus Christ.

First, Rossetti brilliantly combines elements of both the Second and First Coming of Christ. The speaker's God not only cannot be held by heaven or sustained by earth, but shall make them flee away in the fullness of his reign; however, balanced against this is the claim that, in the frozen human world, 'a stable-place sufficed' for God. This pun on 'stable' clearly holds within it both the implication of the precarious – the animal stable in the fierce depths of winter – and the implication of the steady and safe. As so often with Rossetti, she models a theology and poetics that hold both/and rather than either/or. This is a God of paradox and, as such, is the only God worthy of love, worship and respect.

Notably, the Reformed theologian of hymnody Ian Bradley has questioned whether it is right to suggest that heaven cannot hold God, nor earth sustain. However, in 1 Kings 8.27, in Solomon's prayer of dedication for the Temple, he says, 'but will God indeed dwell on the earth? behold, the heaven and heaven of heavens cannot contain thee; how much less this house that I have builded?' While that may offer biblical warrant for Rossetti's claims, I'm more interested in her poetic ambition. Her deceptively simple poetic constructions create imaginative space for visions of God that stretch theology to breaking-point and arguably beyond.

And yet ... just as her theological poetics are about to break into nonsense, she takes us down and down into the simple, the located and the personal, without ever collapsing into sentimentality. Once again, the icy, almost sublime context holds sentiment in check. For, if cherubim worship him, a breastful of milk suffices; if this is a scene that holds within it the possibility of archangels as witnesses, it is not so exalted that a menagerie of wild beasts shivering in the sharpness of midwinter – the very depths of northern bleakness – are excluded from offering their witness too. This is a realm of possibility balanced by the concrete:

Angels and archangels
  May have gathered there,
Cherubim and seraphim
  Thronged the air,
But only His mother
  In her maiden bliss
Worshipped the Beloved
  With a kiss.

Ultimately, then, even if the whole host of heaven may have gathered at this site of wonder and birth, this is a scene shaped by human relationship between mother and child. Only the Virgin worships through the medium of a kiss. This is a kiss of adoration that, theologically, surely counters the final kiss of betrayal from Judas that directs Christ towards his ultimate destiny. Arguably, it is also a kiss of thanksgiving and delight. If one places it in the wider manifesto of Mary's song, her Magnificat sung in Luke 1, it is also a moment of recognition and initiation. There, Mary sings of her child as the one who shall scatter the proud in the conceit of their heart; who shall put down the mighty from their thrones and exalt the lowly. He shall fill the hungry with good things, and send the rich away empty. In this moment between mother and child part of that promise is fulfilled. However, equally in this tender private moment, Mary takes up her central role as teacher, who shall initiate the human Jesus into the Way that shall lead him, in the Beatitudes, to proclaim that the poor and the meek and the hungry are blessed.

It is an extraordinary moment between mother and child. Of course, others are there to worship and adore him, but Rossetti's speaker constructs this scene around the intimacy of Mary's kiss – of her 'maiden bliss'. For that moment, the world of men and power and patriarchal authority is set aside and excluded. Mary and Christ share their peculiar strangeness together. She is mother and yet 'maiden'; Christ is human and yet God. Together they share a kiss of blessing; it is a moment for them alone, and out of it shall come such wondrous fruit.

The rest – the angels and archangels, wise men and shepherds, beast and man – are there as witnesses, not as central characters.

Finally, Rossetti's speaker brings the poem right down to the personal, to each of us. In short, the poem invites the reader to make a response every bit as intimate as that between the Maiden and the God-Child. What an arc this is. It takes us from the sublime to the personal, from the transcendent to the immanent, from the past to the present. This arc leaves us in the realm of the interrogative: 'What can I give Him, / Poor as I am?' The poverty of the speaker – who represents us – is not that of the Blessed Virgin. We cannot offer a kiss as worship, much as one might long to. Yet the fact that a simple maiden can make an offering adequate to the Almighty should encourage us. Rossetti's speaker is hungry to make an offering and is tantalized by hypotheticals. If only she were a shepherd or a wise man, she would know what to do. What on earth can she, can any of us, offer the simple majesty of God among us? There is only one answer: 'my heart'.

To speak of hearts, in poetry and elsewhere, is always to run the risk of kitsch. In this context, however, surely Rossetti's conclusion is correct. The heart is the metaphor *nonpareil* for the very essence of our being. If it has become associated with soppiness and changeability, that is not Rossetti's fault. Perhaps, as a corrective, it might be helpful to recall the famous fourteenth-century story of St Chiara Vengente who, as she was dying, insisted she had 'Christ in her heart'; when she died her body resisted decay for five days, and in light of this miracle the sisters of her convent removed her heart and placed it in a box. A certain Sister Francesca decided to investigate further and cut the heart in two. Inside she found a tiny sculpted crucifix and, alongside, a panoply of miniature items associated with Christ's Passion. These items were wrought from Chiara's flesh itself. Her heart is still on display in a reliquary at Montefalco. If our modern sensibilities find such a story odd or grim, it enacts a vision of the centrality of the heart to faith; it presents us with a vision of what it might mean for that extraordinarily significant organ to be the great gift each of us can offer to God.

Christmas presents people of faith with challenge. Not least among the challenges on offer is a question of how the arrival of God as a baby can be any sort of serious gift at all; when we ask what on earth our own gift to God might look like in return, we find an analogue. 'In the Bleak Midwinter' constructs a series of compelling conundrums that meet those questions with mystery and wonder. The God worshipped by Christians cannot be held by heaven or sustained by earth and yet is – in the moment of Nativity – nothing more than a baby. He is helpless, unable to feed or look after himself. He is so vulnerable that he could not defend himself if we sought to hurt him. Seemingly his only gift is to elicit our love, our kiss, the offering of a beating, changing heart.

Boxing Day/St Stephen's Day

Christmas Day

A baby is a harmless thing
   And wins our hearts with one accord,
And Flower of Babies was their King,
   Jesus Christ our Lord:
Lily of lilies He
Upon His Mother's knee;
Rose of roses, soon to be
Crowned with thorns on leafless tree.

A lamb is innocent and mild
   And merry on the soft green sod;
And Jesus Christ, the Undefiled,
   Is the Lamb of God:
Only spotless He
Upon his Mother's knee;
White and ruddy, soon to be
Sacrificed for you and me.

Nay, lamb is not so sweet a word,
   Nor lily half so pure a name;
Another name our hearts hath stirred,
   Kindling them to flame:
'Jesus' certainly
Is music and melody:
Heart with heart in harmony
Carol we and worship we.

In her copy of Keble's *The Christian Year*, Rossetti added an illustration in response to Keble's poem for St Stephen's Day. It shows the titular martyr, arms outstretched, being stoned to death by three persecutors. It is an extraordinarily dramatic image, showing something of the speculative wonder of Blake, while reflecting a kind of unexpected beauty. Rossetti was no master artist, but she captures something of the simple, mystical beauty held on a day that is part of the Octave of Christmas[24] yet also gestures towards the cost and price of following Christ. Alas, Rossetti herself didn't write a poem specifically for St Stephen's Day. I have therefore used a poem that, as the title suggests, might be better suited for Christmas Day. However, I see connective tissue between Rossetti's 'Christmas Day' and her illustrative addition to Keble's poem for St Stephen's Day: both model mystery with beauty and simplicity; both have a sense of drama. Both engage with conventional images and reformulate them.

Whenever I read the opening line of this poem – 'A baby is a harmless thing' – it gives me pause. Is Rossetti's claim true? Certainly, a baby, especially a new-born, lacks the ready weapons of adults. Yet, in a baby's capacity to win 'our hearts with one accord', I wonder if a baby is the most dangerous, powerful creature in the world. That may be her point, of course, but however one reads her words there is something extraordinary about the new-born. They come to us as gift; they (typically) suspend cynicism and command our attention. Perhaps that's why the Christ-Child is the ultimate signal of the riskiness and wonder of God: he dares to greet us as a creature with no power except to call us into love and care. We adults – or so we presume – have so much power; we certainly can hurt, destroy, make; some of our species have done the most terrible things to babies, infants and children ... and yet ... these strange alien creatures in our midst can call us into new expressions of grace and love.

If 'Christmas Day' challenges us to reflect on the harmlessness or otherwise of babies, it also plays with some conventions about lilies and roses. The poem's speaker calls Christ 'Flower of Babies', a construction that she adds to when she describes him as 'Lily of lilies' and 'Rose of roses'. These are terms that one might more readily connect with the Blessed Virgin than with her Son. Indeed, in the classic carol 'Es ist ein Ros entsprungen', commonly translated as 'Lo, how a rose e'er blooming' or 'A Spotless Rose', the rose is usually associated with the Virgin. In the High Middle Ages, the lily, drawn from the Song of Solomon, was more clearly associated with Mary than with Jesus. Rossetti takes us deeper. Lilies have long been connected with Christ and with kingly lines (especially as the *fleur-de-lys* of the French royal line). Equally, the hymn 'Lo, how a rose e'er blooming' draws on the biblical prophecy that Jesus will emerge from the 'stem of Jesse' (Isaiah 11.1), of which Mary has often been read as the Rose.

In Rossetti's poem, then, we arguably encounter a fascinating play on these traditional themes, emphasizing the deep bond between mother and child. In the images of the flower of babies, lily of lilies and rose of roses, she reminds us of the depth of connection between the Virgin – as Rose and Lily – and Christ as the ultimate Rose. It is an image of Christ that many, influenced by muscular, patriarchal Christianity, might be alarmed by; here is a Christ who is unafraid of closeness to his mother and other classic symbols of femininity. This is a Christ who subverts classic pictures of masculinity and the masculinist God and Christianity. This is the flower who – as Rossetti's speaker reminds us – will ultimately be 'Crowned with thorns on leafless tree'. The wondrously fecund will find its final full-flowering in an ironic manner: on a barren tree.

'Christmas Day' finally turns attention on another familiar representation of Christ: the lamb. Its workings out of this image are unsurprising and more conventional than those of the first stanza, yet they retain a power to shock. The scene of playful innocence – 'merry on the soft green sod' – only underlines the violence that is yet to come. If Christ is set in a sentimental scene – 'spotless He / Upon his Mother's knee' – soon the dandled child shall be sacrificed for us. When set alongside the notion that 'A baby is a harmless thing', the image of sacrifice is almost monstrous. Of course, it is a dimension of the Christian faith that cannot be dismissed. It exists to be wrestled with and responded to. Sacrifice and martyrdom (as in St Stephen's case) are part of the structure of the Christian faith.

The poem takes us from generic nouns – baby, lamb, lily – to a specific name: Jesus. This is the cause of carolling, joy and worship. It is in taking hold of his name that the speaker finds concrete, particular praise and, of course, the possibility of salvation. However, it is also the site of cost. If we are rightly challenged by the notion of a baby or a lamb sacrificed for us, in the end it is a person who fulfils that calling. He is known to us by name. He is no generic saviour figure, but one known to us. This is no salvation in abstract, but one offered to us by one of us, known by name. It is unavoidably costly, potentially devastating, but – in the mystery of God's economy of salvation – the source of hope. How on earth and in heaven that might be is something all of us must wrestle with.

Feast of St John

St. John, Apostle

Earth cannot bar flame from ascending,
Hell cannot bind light from descending,
Death cannot finish life never ending.

Eagle and sun gaze at each other,
Eagle at sun, brother at Brother,
Loving in peace and joy one another.

O St. John, with chains for thy wages,
Strong thy rock where the storm-blast rages,
Rock of refuge, the Rock of Ages.

Rome hath passed with her awful voice,
Earth is passing with all her joys,
Heaven shall pass away with a noise.

So from us all follies that please us,
So from us all falsehoods that ease us,—
Only all saints abide with their Jesus.

Jesus, in love looking down hither,
Jesus, by love draw us up thither,
That we in Thee may abide together.

Given Rossetti's fascination with the Revelation or Apocalypse
of St John (a fascination sufficient to prompt a commentary
on it, *The Face of the Deep*) it is hardly surprising that she
wrote a poem for the saint's day. The poem itself is a sobering
reminder that, right in the heart of the Octave of Christmas,

fearsome and terrible wonder is afoot. Christmas, that most sentimentalized of feasts, resists our shiny glamour and calls us back to reality.

Thus, the poem explodes in a cosmic triplet of real power. It contains a series of assertions that summarize elements of classic doctrine about Christ, delivered from the perspective of John, the 'beloved disciple', evangelist and apocalyptician. In three lines, Rossetti's speaker presents a vision that captures elements of ascension, Christ's breaking open of hell, and the assertion that the God who is killed cannot be destroyed:

> Earth cannot bar flame from ascending,
> Hell cannot bind light from descending,
> Death cannot finish life never ending.

However, in the midst of flame and life, this poem also witnesses to the tradition that holds John as the 'beloved disciple'. As Christ hangs from the cross, love and mutual recognition spread between him and John:

> Eagle and sun gaze at each other,
> Eagle at sun, brother at Brother,
> Loving in peace and joy one another.

Here Rossetti draws on the ancient tradition, found in Augustine's *Tractate 36*, of St John being 'the eagle'. There Augustine calls John 'the preacher of sublime truths, and a contemplator with steady gaze of the inner and eternal light'. He repeats the noted fable that eagle-parents hold their young by their talons, forcing them to gaze directly at the sun; if they hold their sight on the rays of the sun, they are recognized as a true brood. This fable, and Rossetti's version of it, also gestures towards Plato's *Simile of the Cave*, a story that suggests that the true philosopher leaves the cave of shadows to look directly at the Sun of Truth. 'St. John, Apostle', unsurprisingly, doesn't limit itself to pagan myth. The second part of the stanza riffs on John as Eagle and Christ as the Sun; their regard for each other is as brothers. If John's relationship with Christ is a model for all people of faith, then we are invited into sibling relationships shaped by delight and joy in one another. The Christian economy of salvation pulls us towards sibling status, as sisters and brothers with God's Son.

In stanza three, the speaker directly addresses St John. She suggests that Patmos – the place where John's Apocalypse was reputedly composed – is both the 'Rock of refuge' (from Rome, this world, powers and dominions?) and a representation of God himself, the 'Rock of Ages'. In the vision that emerges in 'St. John, Apostle' we participate ever more in the revelation given to St John. Just as in the book of Revelation itself, Rome – presented as symbol of Empire, terrible and inescapable – is passing away, as soon too shall pass the particular joys of the old earth and old heaven. The reader finds herself on the verge of a new world, a world captured both in the human–divine relationship between the disciple and his God on a cross, and also in the vision of the Kingdom breaking in and changing everything. We are, even in the Octave of Christmas, still in the realm of the in-between. All time and space is held together in one place – at the cross, on Patmos – yet shall pass away in God's full revelation. It is extraordinary: exhilarating, terrifying, bewildering, and yet hopeful in its promises.

Finally, Rossetti brings the reader back to the living promise of God, the hope of Christ, on this the third day of Christmas:

So from us all follies that please us,
So from us all falsehoods that ease us,—
Only all saints abide with their Jesus.

Jesus, in love looking down hither,
Jesus, by love draw us up thither,
That we in Thee may abide together.

The speaker posits that 'Only all saints abide with their Jesus'. This might dishearten some readers. Who, among us, can count as a saint? We are not John, the beloved and faithful one. However, we may call to Jesus from the foot of the cross, standing alongside John; we may stand with other witnesses gathered around the crib of Jesus. We may invite Jesus to look down and draw us up. The polarities are reversed. At Christmas time we may imagine it is we who look down at the crib, at the vulnerable baby; but this child holds the height of the cross in his being. He looks down from the 'cross-crib' with love, and wishes to draw us up as his beloved, with John and with all the saints.

Holy Innocents

Holy Innocents

They scarcely waked before they slept,
  They scarcely wept before they laughed;
  They drank indeed death's bitter draught,
But all its bitterest dregs were kept
And drained by Mothers while they wept.

From Heaven the speechless Infants speak:
  Weep not (they say), our Mothers dear,
  For swords nor sorrows come not here.
Now we are strong who were so weak,
And all is ours we could not seek.

We bloom among the blooming flowers,
  We sing among the singing birds;
  Wisdom we have who wanted words:
Here morning knows not evening hours,
All's rainbow here without the showers.

And softer than our Mother's breast,
  And closer than our Mother's arm,
  Is here the Love that keeps us warm
And broods above our happy next.
Dear Mothers, come: for Heaven is best.

Holy Innocents

Unspotted lambs to follow the one Lamb,
  Unspotted doves to wait on the one Dove;
To whom Love saith, 'Be with Me where I am,'
  And lo! their answer unto Love is love.

For tho' I know not any note they know,
  Nor know one word of all their song above,
I know Love speaks to them, and even so
  I know the answer unto Love is love.

Rossetti wrote a number of poems for the feast of the Holy
Innocents. Two are offered above. Perhaps the fact she wrote
several for this feast indicates that, like any of us who call our-
selves sensitive, attentive Christians, it is a feast that demands
determined, careful attention. It should trouble us. It should
generate silence and words. It should not simply be pushed
away as an inconvenience during our Christmas celebrations.
It needs to be addressed. Indeed, in the popular spirituality of
medieval mystery plays it was addressed, most notably in the
haunting words of the still-sung 'Coventry Carol'. However,
the Feast of the Holy Innocents has slipped out of the domin-
ant narratives of the Christmas period. We are inclined to
reject it as unsuitable for our modern festive sensibilities; our
Christmas is shaped around cosy images of family where senti-
mental images of childhood rule. However, Holy Innocents is
the feast that, arguably, draws us back to our species' failings
more than any other; in it we encounter how power and fear
prevent and frustrate the call to be fully human.

The first of the two poems explored here on the theme of
the Holy Innocents, written in about 1877, presents sentiments
that perhaps are at odds with our (post-)modern sensibilities. It
dares to speak on behalf of the slaughtered innocents, placing
words into their mouths. Such lyric gestures can seem patron-
izing and tasteless, especially in the shadow of the Shoah and
the serial slaughter of innocent lives that marked the twentieth
century. If we do not quite say, with Theodor Adorno, 'there

can be no (lyric) poetry after Auschwitz', many struggle with poetic gesture that appropriates slaughter for lyric and theological ends. To claim that the Holy Innocents are 'with the angels' has – in contemporary contexts – a rather sickly and lazy feel. In the face of mass slaughter, such popular piety can seem overly sentimental and tractionless.

However, Rossetti's poetics are surprisingly resilient in this first poem, supplying intriguing ironies, especially at the outset. If our modern readings of the Holy Innocents might emphasize horror or violence, she emphasizes near-paradox:

> They scarcely waked before they slept,
> They scarcely wept before they laughed;
> They drank indeed death's bitter draught,
> But all its bitterest dregs were kept
> And drained by Mothers while they wept.

The claim that they scarcely wept before they laughed is heartbreaking. It conjures in one line an image of crying infants – perhaps crying in the face of their terrifying attackers – before dying and being received by God. However, there is a further implication: if this life is a vale of tears, they have also been spared life's trials. Here irony piles on irony because the speaker acknowledges that death is bitter, and life, even if marked by tears, is still life. The 'innocents' have simultaneously been spared and denied. The costs of life lived in the lee of tears is only deferred, not escaped. The pain is passed from those whose lives have been cut short on to their mothers. The bitter dregs of death are drunk by them; they live and yet they also die in their children.

Given this opening, is Rossetti's potentially gloopy second stanza rather more justified? I think it is. Even if one must ultimately deal with an increasingly questionable sentiment as the poem progresses, leading ultimately to the conclusion, 'Dear Mothers, come: for Heaven is best', the opening stanza holds back the sentiment for a while. The notion of 'speechless Infants' speaking is, of course, fantastical, yet it perhaps offers an appropriate response to the monstrousness of their slaying. Their refrain – that violence cannot reach into heaven – offers a substantive response to a world of silencing. It may seem inadequate in a world where slaughter is normalized, but I do not find it worthy of mockery.

The second, shorter poem shared for this day offers, perhaps, a more mysterious and nuanced response to the problem of the slaughter of the Holy Innocents. One of the puzzles presented by the Holy Innocents – as saints – is that they are slaughtered while Christ goes free. For some, this makes the Innocents mere 'collateral damage', for the sake of the divine plan. Rossetti offers a subtler picture:

> Unspotted lambs to follow the one Lamb,
>   Unspotted doves to wait on the one Dove;
> To whom Love saith, 'Be with Me where I am,'
>   And lo! their answer unto Love is love.

She does not offer a justification for slaughter; rather, she sets it in the context of the sacrificial 'Lamb' and the 'Dove' of Grace – that is, of Christ himself. In the world of this short lyric poem, this context presents the Lamb/Dove as having gone ahead of the Holy Innocents. This is an intriguing play on time and space. In terms of 'human' diachronic time, the Innocents are slaughtered and the Holy Family escape to Egypt; Rossetti's speaker, however, suggests that in divine time Christ is always going ahead and is always ahead of us. Human time is linear, but God's time brings another dimension. The God who is Love says that 'there is no place beyond me and there is no place that I have not gone before you get there'. He says this not only to the slaughtered Innocents, but to all. The violence inflicted on the Innocents was cruel and wicked, but it is not beyond God. The crucified God stands for all those slaughtered without justice and his story reaches back and forth through all time and space.

This runs the risk of being a complacent answer. Love, as I have explored already, can so readily be deployed in a lazy manner. Rossetti is too Victorian for that. She is too committed to an Anglo-Catholic poetics. Her conclusion is plaintive, simple and affecting:

> For tho' I know not any note they know,
>   Nor know one word of all their song above,
> I know Love speaks to them, and even so
>   I know the answer unto Love is love.

I do not read this stanza in sentimental terms. I read it as determined resistance to a world that would either cynically prefer to avoid its own violence or like to claim an undeserved virtue. Love is costly, exposing and tough. In the final reckoning, though, it is all that shall save us from the abyss.

Fifth Day of Christmas

Christmastide

Love came down at Christmas,
   Love all lovely, Love Divine;
Love was born at Christmas,
   Star and Angels gave the sign.

Worship we the Godhead,
   Love Incarnate, Love Divine;
Worship we our Jesus:
   But wherewith for sacred sign?

Love shall be our token,
   Love shall be yours and love be mine,
Love to God and to all men,
   Love for plea and gift and sign.

'Love Came Down at Christmas' – as 'Christmastide' is more commonly known – has sparked the imaginations of composers without ever quite achieving the public recognition it deserves. Harold Darke and John Rutter are just two of the prominent composers who have set the poem to music. If it is always going to sit in the shadow of 'In the Bleak Midwinter', it none the less holds its own music and theological interest.

One way of approaching this poem's lyric effects is to consider how Rossetti disobeys contemporary poetic conventions. *Contemporary Poetry 101* instructs the beginning poet to avoid abstract nouns. The emphasis is always on forming concrete images in specific settings. By contrast, Rossetti makes

'Love' the frame on which to hold this poem. To do so may leave readers – especially those who find themselves on the margins of faith – asking, 'Whose love?', 'What kind of love?', yet Rossetti more than gets away with her abstraction. The concrete context is provided by another word that for some is equally as nebulous as 'love': 'Christmas'. 'Love came down at Christmas' is simultaneously strange, abstract, yet utterly grounded in the particularities of good poetry: it leaves its readers in the company of Christ.

The idea that love might 'descend' or 'come down' from heaven is one to conjure with. It immediately implies that before this incarnational moment, there was an impairment, a lack. Love was, in some sense, absent or less present. The construction invites the reader to re-interrogate the texts of the Tanakh/Old Testament for the traces of God's love and its limits; this, I hope, will lead to a variety of conclusions – not simply that the world was so broken before Christ that it was almost of secondary value. The paradox of Christianity is that we say, with the writer of John's Gospel, that the Word was from the beginning; in the incarnation, however, we see the fulfilment of the Law of Love, its utterly human face made present. If 'Love was born at Christmas' – a phrase that should arrest us with its bold claim, as Rossetti's speaker indicates – at the same time 'Worship we the Godhead'.

We are creatures limited in time and space, who require language, symbol and sign in order to navigate even the slightest glimpses of eternity. Therefore,

Love shall be our token,
   Love shall be yours and love be mine,
Love to God and to all men,
   Love for plea and gift and sign.

In the midst of human limit, love supplies the means that enables us to orient towards God's eternity. As humans, we are caught between what the body can teach us and what symbol reveals, for we are creatures of both flesh and language.

In Christ – a body, a particular person called Jesus – we find our specific, definitive guide into the shape of love. In Jesus Christ, love is no longer nebulous or abstract. We meet love in the gurgle and cry of a baby, but also in the facts of a baby's incapacity and vulnerability. We must change his 'nappy', we must hold him to our breast and feed him.

From this one body, shall all things come – salvation, rejoicing, redemption. Love comes among us and – as 'Christmastide' claims – a trinity of good things are thereby revealed: love for plea (for through Jesus we shall enter the courts of judgement with him as our witness and friend); love for gift (for in Christ we see that all is gift from the One who creates and loves all); and love for sign. The sign is sacramental: it holds within it grace, but it also directs us to the riches of the universe and the Godhead himself. The character of this sacramental sign – this Word of God – is surprise. For, what the baby Jesus reveals is not so much God's judgement, or justice, or even grace, but Love. God is Love and in this truth is joy abounding.

Sixth Day of Christmas

A Christmas Carol (1859)

Before the paling of the stars
   Before the winter morn
Before the earliest cockcrow
   Jesus Christ was born:
Born in a stable
   Cradled in a manger,
In the world His Hands had made
   Born a Stranger.

Priest and King lay fast asleep
   In Jerusalem,
Young and old lay fast asleep
   In crowded Bethlehem:
Saint and Angel Ox and Ass,
   Kept a watch together,
Before the Christmas daybreak
   In the winter weather.

Jesus on His Mother's breast
   In the stable cold,
Spotless Lamb of God was He
   Shepherd of the Fold:
Let us kneel with Mary Maid
   With Joseph bent and hoary
With Saint and Angel Ox and Ass,
   To hail the King of Glory.

When one places this Christmas carol alongside the mastery of 'In the Bleak Midwinter' or 'Love Came Down at Christmas', it comes off slightly worse for wear. Its imagery can strike us as a little second-hand, hackneyed and lacking in boldness. In 'A Christmas Carol', there is none of the strange boldness of a line like 'Love was born at Christmas' or the terse conditionality of 'Angels and Archangels may have gathered there'. However, it doesn't follow that this poem/carol is unworthy of attention. Christmas provides profound riches, but does not necessarily supply endless novelty.

Thus, this poem rehearses some familiar themes and tropes, handled with typical aplomb by Rossetti. In stanzas two and three, she unfolds a classic scene. She conjures readily appreciated images of a slumbering elite – in more ways than one – in Jerusalem, as well as the sleeping census-attendees crowded into little Bethlehem. In this poem, the sacred – 'Saint and Angel' – mingles easily with the profane – 'Ox and Ass'. It is what we have come to expect at Christmastime. Equally, this scene unfolds in a cold, winter context, a northern European nativity, in which mother and child perform their appointed roles, and Rossetti exhorts us to our devotions:

> Let us kneel with Mary Maid
>   With Joseph bent and hoary
> With Saint and Angel Ox and Ass,
>   To hail the King of Glory.

This is all most conventional. However, given that 'A Christmas Carol' was written by Rossetti, it contains some remarkable flourishes, not least its fascinating opening stanza:

> Before the paling of the stars
>   Before the winter morn
> Before the earliest cockcrow
>   Jesus Christ was born:
> Born in a stable
>   Cradled in a manger,

In the world His Hands had made
Born a Stranger.

Her characteristic use of anaphora (the repetition of a word) as she repeats 'Before' pushes the reader back and back in time, almost to that famous phrase of John, 'In the beginning was the Word'. The reader is left in no doubt about the primacy of Jesus Christ. As ever with Rossetti, there is playfulness and theological astuteness in her lines. We move back through the cosmic ('the stars'), the seasons ('winter morn') and other natural phenomena ('the earliest cockcrow') to the primacy of Christ; of course, this cockcrow also gestures towards St Peter's denial of Christ before his trial and condemnation. As Christ says in the Gospels, 'Before the cock crows, you shall deny me three times.' Time is further played with when the poem's speaker reminds us that Christ 'cradled in a manger' has also made the world. The final line is pungent and is as potent in our time as in any: this child, born in vulnerability, is also maker of all reality. He comes as alien and stranger: creator and yet created, the ground of all being, and yet an easily broken human being. This is the strangest moment in all history.

New Year's Eve and New Year's Day

Old and New Year Ditties

1

New Year met me somewhat sad:
  Old Year leaves me tired,
Stripped of favourite things I had,
  Baulked of much desired:
Yet farther on my road today,
God willing, farther on my way.

New Year coming on apace,
  What have you to give me?
Bring you scathe, or bring you grace,
Face me with an honest face;
  You shall not deceive me:
Be it good or ill, be it what you will,
It needs shall help me on my road,
My rugged way to heaven, please God.

2

Watch with me, men, women, and children dear,
You whom I love, for whom I hope and fear,
Watch with me this last vigil of the year.
Some hug their business, some their pleasure scheme;
Some seize the vacant hour to sleep or dream;
Heart locked in heart some kneel and watch apart.

Watch with me, blessed spirits, who delight
All thro' the holy night to walk in white,

Or take your ease after the long-drawn fight.
I know not if they watch with me: I know
They count this eve of resurrection slow,
And cry 'How long?' with urgent utterance strong.

Watch with me, Jesus, in my loneliness:
Tho' others say me nay, yet say Thou yes;
Tho' others pass me by, stop Thou to bless.
Yea, Thou dost stop with me this vigil night;
Tonight of pain, to-morrow of delight:
I, Love, am Thine; Thou, Lord my God, art mine.

3

Passing away, saith the World, passing away:
Chances, beauty, and youth, sapped day by day:
Thy life never continueth in one stay.
Is the eye waxen dim, is the dark hair changing to grey
That hath won neither laurel nor bay?
I shall clothe myself in Spring and bud in May:
Thou, root-stricken, shalt not rebuild thy decay
On my bosom for aye.
Then I answered: Yea.

Passing away, saith my Soul, passing away:
With its burden of fear and hope, of labour and play,
Hearken what the past doth witness and say:
Rust in thy gold, a moth is in thine array,
A canker is in thy bud, thy leaf must decay.
At midnight, at cockcrow, at morning, one certain day
Lo the Bridegroom shall come and shall not delay;
Watch thou and pray.
Then I answered: Yea.

Passing away, saith my God, passing away:
Winter passeth after the long delay:
New grapes on the vine, new figs on the tender spray,
Turtle calleth turtle in Heaven's May.
Tho' I tarry, wait for Me, trust Me, watch and pray:

Arise, come away, night is past and lo it is day,
My love, My sister, My spouse, thou shalt hear Me say.
Then I answered: Yea.

This trinity of New Year poems, written over three or so years in the late 1850s, presents an opportunity not only to offer thoughts for two days' worth of reflections, but to step in a slightly different direction during Christmastide. Some will be surprised at this step, not least because I have consistently reiterated Rossetti's fascination with divine time, rather than its secular variety. However, as these poems – or 'ditties' as she calls them – demonstrate, Rossetti was intrigued (certainly during the early stages of her career) by the ordinary markers of time and their possibilities.

If the notion of New Year falling on 31 December/1 January is secular, in Christian terms Advent signals the new liturgical year. Rossetti here is attentive to the intersections between the eschatological and the ending of the profane year.[25] In the second of these three poems, she writes:

Watch with me, men, women, and children dear,
You whom I love, for whom I hope and fear,
Watch with me this last vigil of the year.

This not only models an echo of the watching and waiting that marks Advent, it is also a gesture towards the religious notion of vigil – a concept that plays out strongly in the idea of the eve of a holy day or feast day. Vigil gestures towards the idea of seeking to stay awake when one might ordinarily be expected to be asleep. In this stanza, the speaker hints at a sense of ordinary holiness found, however dimly, in secular time.

Secular time itself lies in the shadow of divine time. Indeed, Rossetti makes this connection between the turning of the old year and Christian ideas of the vigil, of watching and waiting for new life, explicit in the two verses that follow:

Watch with me, blessed spirits, who delight
All thro' the holy night to walk in white,
Or take your ease after the long-drawn fight.
I know not if they watch with me: I know
They count this eve of resurrection slow,
And cry 'How long?' with urgent utterance strong.

Watch with me, Jesus, in my loneliness:
Tho' others say me nay, yet say Thou yes;
Tho' others pass me by, stop Thou to bless.
Yea, Thou dost stop with me this vigil night;
Tonight of pain, to-morrow of delight:
I, Love, am Thine; Thou, Lord my God, art mine.

The speaker's sense of isolation in this vigil is plaintive: not
only does she indicate her uncertainty that 'blessed spirits'
(which may represent the dear departed, or the saints or the
angels) 'watch with me', but she asks Jesus to 'watch with me
... in my loneliness'.

There is a sense, then, of a noble and holy watching and
waiting. This is the watching and waiting that echoes that of
the knight or the nun, preparing to be consecrated. This lone-
liness is costly – shaped by 'Tonight of pain' but a 'to-morrow
of delight'. It is a personal consecration that is also part of the
wider patterns of life in which anyone can encounter both long
nights of pain and doubt, and 'daylight' that is shaped by hope.
This second of the 'Old and New Year Ditties' holds, in its
three stanzas, a reminder that – in Rossetti's picture of God's
economy – the natural turning of the year can be read in reli-
gious terms. There is no sharp separation, but a symbiosis that
indicates that God is ecologically caught up in every dimension
of creation; if we are prepared to be attentive we shall see him
alive within it.

The death of the old year – as Rossetti explores in the first
of the ditties – also holds within it an implication of stripping
away ('Stripped of favourite things I had, / Baulked of much
desired'); there is something penitential in this, a removal of the

unnecessary yet treasured things of the world before it blooms again in spring. It is a natural process as much as a theological one. Again, we see an echo of or gesture towards the religious in this natural movement. However, given that we are still in the Christmas season, there is something more. It indicates that, even in the midst of feast, there is within Christianity an honest appraisal of and call towards fast and self-denial. There is an astringency pregnant even within abundance.

The final of the three ditties brings these themes front and centre through the imagery of 'passing away'. Rossetti's speaker personifies the 'World', the 'Soul', and allows God to speak for himself. Each voice is permitted to comment on the impact of time on flesh, youth, promise and fecundity. The world might 'clothe myself in Spring and bud in May' but mortal collapse is inescapable: 'Thou, root-stricken, shalt not rebuild thy decay'. The world invites its inhabitants to say 'yea' to the facts that we shall turn to grey, then to dust. The speaker's soul presents a different challenge. The burdens of the soul are 'passing away', but – as soul – the speaker confronts the question of God's eternity and Kingdom. At every point in time – 'At midnight, at cockcrow, at morning, one certain day' – God is arriving ('Lo the Bridegroom shall come and shall not delay'). The appropriate response is clear: 'Watch thou and pray. / Then I answered: Yea.'

The speaker's God is given the final word: all is 'Passing away ... passing away'. This includes nature's seasons, as much as the theological significations. Figs and grapes on vines hold natural as well as theological meanings. All this, the speaker is told, is passing away. In the midst of the end of all things – of the old year, of old identities and of the promise of youth – the speaker is asked to trust. It is an invitation offered to each of us:

Tho' I tarry, wait for Me, trust Me, watch and pray:
Arise, come away, night is past and lo it is day,
My love, My sister, My spouse, thou shalt hear Me say.
Then I answered: Yea.

Towards Epiphany

'If I Were a Wise Man'

Ninth Day of Christmas

A Christmas Carol,
for my Godchildren (1856)

The shepherds had an Angel,
  The wise men had a star,
But what have I, a little child,
  To guide me home from far,
Where glad stars sing together
  And singing angels are?—

Lord Jesus is my Guardian,
  So I can nothing lack:
The lambs lie in His Bosom
  Along life's dangerous track:
The wilful lambs that go astray
  He bleeding fetches back.

Lord Jesus is my Guiding Star,
  My Beacon Light in heaven:
He leads me step by step along
  The path of life uneven:
He, True Light, leads me to that land
  Whose day shall be as seven.

Those shepherds through the lonely night
  Sat watching by their sheep,
Until they saw the heavenly host
  Who neither tire nor sleep
All singing 'Glory glory'
  In festival they keep.

Christ watches me, His little lamb,
    Cares for me day and night,
That I may be His Own in heaven:
    So angels clad in white
Shall sing their 'Glory glory'
    For my sake in the height.

The wise men left their country
    To journey morn by morn
With gold and frankincense and myrrh,
    Because the Lord was born:
God sent a star to guide them
    And sent a dream to warn.

My life is like their journey,
    Their star is like God's Book;
I must be like those good wise men
    With heavenward heart and look:
But shall I give no gifts to God?—
    What precious gifts they took!

Lord, I will give my love to Thee,
    Than gold much costlier,
Sweeter to Thee than frankincense,
    More prized than choicest myrrh:
Lord, make me dearer day by day,
    Day by day holier;

Nearer and dearer day by day:
    Till I my voice unite,
And I sing my 'Glory glory'
    With angels clad in white;
All 'Glory glory' given to Thee
    Through all the heavenly height.

We are deep into Christmas now, and perhaps we have grown sick of its abundance and festal joy. We may feel Christmas is effectively behind us. Indeed, by now, the secular version of it insists it is. We are now in the new year, and we are in the midst of sales, people have started diets and many of us are planning for what is yet to come. Perhaps, some supermarkets already have displays out for the next consumer feast – Valentine's Day or even Easter.

Today's poem, as the subtitle suggests, is a carol written for children. Her brother William Michael wrote, in his *The Poetical Works of Christina Georgina Rossetti*, that 'Christina, from time to time, acted as godmother to various children – mostly, I think, children of poor people in the neighbourhood of Christ Church, Albany Street, Regent's Park.' This information adds a little poignancy to the poem. However, even if we are passionately maintaining our Christmas feast, we may wish to add our voices to the speaker's wistful, longing voice in the opening stanza:

> The shepherds had an Angel,
>   The wise men had a star,
> But what have I, a little child,
>   To guide me home from far,
> Where glad stars sing together
>   And singing angels are?—

What have each of us to guide us home from afar? Perhaps we are weighed down with responsibilities – indeed, perhaps others depend on us so much that we can only view ourselves as adults. However, through the lens of the Almighty we are all children. Adult-children, perhaps, but still children who need a guide to draw us safely home. Perhaps those poor godchildren of Rossetti needed such a guide more than most.

The guide offered by the poem's speaker is, unsurprisingly, 'Lord Jesus'. Even with the best will in the world, most of us don't have the courage and trust to admit our need for him. Even fewer of us would risk making ourselves look foolish by framing our need in terms of our being as little children. When we speak of 'Lord Jesus' perhaps our minds rush, especially at Christmas, to 'little Lord Jesus' in 'Away in a Manger'. This is not a picture of Christ that many grown-ups are going to sit easily with. We, understandably, do not want to infantilize ourselves by over-indulgence in sentimental Christmas pictures.

However, there is always tension in the Christmas feast. If in an honest and authentic life there shall inevitably be shadow and pain, and threat, there is something to be said for embracing an image of ourselves as children in need of Lord Jesus. For it invites us to dethrone our often fake images of ourselves as powerful and competent; and even if we be powerful and competent, that is rarely the point at which God can actually meet and transform us. Are we prepared to say, with Rossetti's speaker and the poor children whom she addresses, that 'Christ watches me, His little lamb, / Cares for me day and night'? Not in the manner of one who is complacent or smug, but as one who is exposed to the often cruel and disturbing realities of the world. What would we be like if we were to assert Christ's simple care and love in a world where lambs – among whom one would surely count the children of the poor around Regent's Park in the 1850s – are so readily killed?

The notion of 'journey' has become over-exposed, worn-thin and commonplace. It has become cliché because it is a useful metaphor for pilgrimage. This poem invites the reader to join his story to the speaker's when she says, of the magi, 'My life is like their journey, / Their star is like God's Book'. Our journey through Advent and Christmas is not to be compared to the journey of a wannabe celebrity in a TV talent show, in which one would be required to utter how grateful one is to have been voted for by a judgemental and labile public. The Christian pilgrim's journey is not towards fame or celebrity. It is towards truth and into truth; it will reveal who we are rather than who we want to be. It will show up the foundation of the world as love and we shall be called into worship. Even if this poem might work best as a carol for children, I do not see grounds why anyone mature in faith should be ashamed to sing:

Nearer and dearer day by day:
   Till I my voice unite,
And I sing my 'Glory glory'
   With angels clad in white;
All 'Glory glory' given to Thee
   Through all the heavenly height.[26]

Tenth Day of Christmas

Christmas Carols (1887)

1

Whoso hears a chiming for Christmas at the nighest,
   Hears a sound like Angels chanting in their glee,
Hears a sound like palm boughs waving in the highest,
   Hears a sound like ripple of a crystal sea.

Sweeter than a prayer-bell for a saint in dying,
   Sweeter than a death-bell for a saint at rest,
Music struck in Heaven with earth's faint replying
   'Life is good, and death is good, for Christ is Best.'

2

A holy heavenly chime
Rings fulness in of time,
And on His Mother's breast
Our Lord God ever-Blest
Is laid a Babe at rest.

Stoop, Spirits unused to stoop,
Swoop, Angels, flying swoop,
Adoring as you gaze,
Uplifting hymns of praise:—
'Grace to the Full of Grace!'

The cave is cold and strait
To hold the angelic state:
More strait it is, more cold,

To foster and infold
Its Maker one hour old.

Thrilled thro' with awestruck love,
Meek Angels poised above,
To see their God, look down:
'What, is there never a Crown
For Him in swaddled gown?

'How comes He soft and weak
With such a tender cheek,
With such a soft small hand?—
The very Hand which spann'd
Heaven when its girth was plann'd.

'How comes He with a voice
Which is but baby-noise?—
That Voice which spake with might
—"Let there be light"—and light
Sprang out before our sight.

'What need hath He of flesh
Made flawless now afresh?
What need of human heart?—
Heart that must bleed and smart,
Choosing the better part.

'But see: His gracious smile
Dismisses us a while
To serve Him in His kin.
Haste we, make haste, begin
To fetch His brethren in.'

Like stars they flash and shoot,
The Shepherds they salute:
'Glory to God' they sing:
'Good news of peace we bring,
For Christ is born a King.'

3

Lo! newborn Jesus
   Soft and weak and small,
Wrapped in baby's bands
By His Mother's hands,
   Lord God of all.

Lord God of Mary,
   Whom His Lips caress
While He rocks to rest
On her milky breast
   In helplessness.

Lord God of shepherds
   Flocking through the cold,
Flocking through the dark
To the only Ark,
   The only Fold.

Lord God of all things
   Be they near or far,
Be they high or low;
Lord of storm and snow,
   Angel and star.

Lord God of all men,—
   My Lord and my God!
Thou who lovest me,
Keep me close to Thee
   By staff and rod.

Lo! newborn Jesus
   Loving great and small,
Love's free Sacrifice,
Opening Arms and Eyes
   To one and all.

Behind the famous carols, sung relentlessly during this season, there are many more or less well-concealed traditions and songs.

I've already spoken of the 'Coventry Carol'. The Coventry Mysteries also supply a carol of sublime beauty known as 'The Cherry-Tree Carol', and the medieval era's popular piety further generated carols of the excellence of the 'Salutation Carol', which offers an arresting take on the Annunciation (and was later set to music by Ralph Vaughan Williams). There is also what might be called the modern 'working-class' carol traditions represented by those who sang (and still sing) 'Sheffield Carols'. These carols use local folk tunes for familiar carols, as well as offering original words and songs of their own.

This trinity of carols falls outside those regularly sung during the festive season. Their interest lies in how they intersect with classic, familiar carols as well as relate to others from less well-known sources. In the 'Sheffield Carols' tradition, there is a setting of 'While Shepherds Watched Their Flocks' called 'Sweet Bells'. It is almost insanely catchy. Like 'Ding Dong Merrily On High', the carol 'Sweet Bells' riffs on the power of bells and their chiming during the festive season. The first (and, to an extent, the second) of Rossetti's carols joins these other carols in riffing on the power of bells and chimes:

Whoso hears a chiming for Christmas at the nighest,
    Hears a sound like Angels chanting in their glee,
Hears a sound like palm boughs waving in the highest,
    Hears a sound like ripple of a crystal sea.

Sweeter than a prayer-bell for a saint in dying,
    Sweeter than a death-bell for a saint at rest,
Music struck in Heaven with earth's faint replying
    'Life is good, and death is good, for Christ is Best.'

She is clearly aware of the extraordinary power of bells to lift the mood or draw attention away from earthly concerns, so that we might hear the 'Angels chanting in their glee'. For many of us who grew up in the English countryside there is something reassuring and transporting about bells. They are almost unutterably English, with the largest of bells often forged next to the towers in which they are set. In some places one can still see the pits where the bells were constructed. In our relentlessly noisy urban and suburban world, and even in the contemporary countryside, it is difficult to appreciate the power of bells – to summon, to comfort, to warn and to sing. As I write, thousands of cars pass outside my house urgently trying to get to the city centre. The noise is terrific. If the church where I'm rector had a complement of bells they should not be heard over it. In Rossetti's world – whether urban or rural – there was still sufficient silence in most places for the power of bells, in both their chiming and their silence, to be heard. No wonder they were used to alert people to the threat of potential invasion, or to summon mourners and worshippers to church.

Rossetti's poem here makes me think of Dorothy L. Sayers's famous Wimsey book, *The Nine Tailors*. It is set in the Fens, and bells and campanology play a central role in the plot. Rossetti's speaker, as with Sayers, acknowledges the peculiar power of bells to communicate, as well as their role in liturgical gesture: the Christmas peal draws our attention to angels singing 'Glory to God in the Highest and peace to men on earth', but their communicative power is not limited to rejoicing. In traditional contexts, bells function as signals for impending death and for death itself. Bells are heralds of the Kingdom yet to come, at both a personal and a global level. My own grandmother, growing up in late Victorian rural England, had the job of tolling the death-bell as the deceased were brought into church. As Sayers's Lord Peter – an expert on campanology – acknowledges, 'there's something queer about bells'. Indeed, as Sayers rather wonderfully expresses it, 'the bells, with mute black mouths gaping downwards, brooded in their ancient places'. Bells and chimes connect us with something stranger than ourselves and – even today when we are all plugged into iPods and screaming at one another as we commute to work or feel overwhelmed by noise – the chime of bells can speak to us of glory, and mortality and of wonder. Of that Rossetti was fully appraised, as was Dorothy L. Sayers when she wrote in *The Nine Tailors*:

The ringers were practising their Christmas peal; it drifted through the streaming rain with an aching and intolerable melancholy, like the noise of the bells of a drowned city pulsing up through the overwhelming sea.

Eleventh Day of Christmas

A Hymn for Christmas Day

The Shepherds watch their flocks by night,
Beneath the moon's unclouded light,
All around is calm and still,
Save the murm'ring of the rill:
When lo! a form of light appears,
And on the awe-struck Shepherds' ears
Are words, of peace and comfort flowing
From lips with love celestial glowing.
Spiritual forms are breaking
Through the gloom, their voices taking
Part in the adoring song
Of the bright angelic throng.
Wondering the Shepherds bend
Their steps to Bethlehem, and wend
To a poor and crowded inn:—
Tremblingly their way they win
To the stable, where they find
The Redeemer of mankind,
Just born into this world of danger,
Lying in an humble manger.
And they spread abroad each word
Which that joyful night they'd heard,
And they glorified the name
Of their gracious God, Who came
Himself to save from endless woe
The offspring of this world below.

It is, perhaps, a little naughty to include a poem written for Christmas Day so late in the festive season. However, if this feast demonstrates a range of registers and movements – including Holy Innocents, the feast of John, as well as the secular facts of New Year – as we prepare to depart the Christmas season and focus on Epiphany, it is worth rehearsing once again the festal heart of the matter. As I have sought to explore through my commentaries on Rossetti's work, there is a profound sense in which being Christian is to commit oneself to a cyclical life, where one returns again and again to beginnings. Terminuses are places to commence as well as to end.

'A Hymn for Christmas Day' holds echoes and suggestions of other, more memorable carols. The opening line gestures towards the older hymn 'While Shepherds Watched Their Flocks by Night' (which, apparently, was the only officially sanctioned carol in the Church of England until the 1970s), while line three is suggestive of the English translation of 'Silent Night' (although it is worth remembering that this poem was composed in the 1840s, a good decade before the English translation of 'Silent Night' was published). If these connections imply that 'A Hymn for Christmas Day' is a modest contribution to Rossetti's oeuvre, it doesn't follow that it lacks interest.

Among the notable moments in this poem is the speaker's claim that the shepherds 'find / The Redeemer of mankind, / Just born into this world of danger, / Lying in an humble manger.' If the rhyme 'danger' and 'manger' is straightforward, the immediacy that Rossetti generates in the line 'Just born into this world of danger' is not. Having set up a tender, pastoral scene – shepherds watching flocks, a moonlit night calm and still, with the added details of a babbling brook ('murm'ring of the rill') – the poem's speaker balances the theological and existential in the arrival of the saviour. The speaker is clear that the child in the humble manger is 'the Redeemer of mankind'. However, this redeemer arrives into a 'world of danger'. What might be construed as nothing more than a piece of sentimental pastoralia is – unquestionably – set in a hard-edged reality. Rossetti and her contemporaries would – in ways we can barely imagine – understand the fraught facts of nativity in a world with limited medical facilities. Though she was never a mother herself, she would have been only too aware of the unsanitary conditions many children were born into, and the risks to mothers of simply giving birth.

Of course, this 'world of danger' extends far and wide beyond the immediate problems faced by any new-born or mother. It is a phrase that is worthy of remembrance, not only during Christmastide, but across the year. It has traction in season and out, for people of faith and of none. In another Victorian carol, 'O Little Town of Bethlehem', the writer Phillips Brooks speaks of 'this world of sin'. It has pungency and piety, but in these chastened times I prefer Rossetti's 'world of danger'. It captures the facts of contemporary life in a way that does not require a doctrinaire commitment to Christian theology. It holds the sense of peril that 'sin' does, but it also engages us with the perils of the natural world and the violence that is present in our private lives, in political gesture and in international catastrophe. How a world of danger still longs for its redeemer.

As we prepare for the feast of the Epiphany and – in some traditions – the end of the feast of Christmas, it is worth hearing once again of the faithfulness of the shepherds, those fascinating witnesses of the Nativity. Some have claimed that they represent the outcasts, suggesting that – because of their profession – shepherds were unable to fulfil the ritual requirements of the Jewish faith; others have drawn attention to the way shepherds are the heart of biblical faith, with God and Christ being identified as the shepherd of the flock. Shepherds, perhaps, are interesting because they can be read in so many ways. Yet, as the poem's speaker brings out, in the moment of nativity they were blessed and were faithful to God's call. They met their saviour as all Christians are invited to do, and did not fail to sing God's song:

And they spread abroad each word
Which that joyful night they'd heard,
And they glorified the name
Of their gracious God, Who came
Himself to save from endless woe
The offspring of this world below.

Epiphany

Epiphany

'Lord Babe, if Thou art He
We sought for patiently,
Where is Thy court?
Hither may prophecy and star resort;
Men heed not their report.'—
   'Bow down and worship, righteous man:
   This Infant of a span
   Is He man sought for since the world began!'—
'Then, Lord, accept my gold, too base a thing
For Thee, of all kings King.'—

'Lord Babe, despite Thy youth
I hold Thee of a truth
Both Good and Great:
But wherefore dost Thou keep so mean a state,
Low-lying desolate?'—
   'Bow down and worship, righteous seer:
   The Lord our God is here
   Approachable, Who bids us all draw near.'—
'Wherefore to Thee I offer frankincense,
Thou Sole Omnipotence.'—

'But I have only brought
Myrrh; no wise afterthought
Instructed me
To gather pearls or gems, or choice to see
Coral or ivory.'—

'Not least thine offering proves thee wise:
For myrrh means sacrifice,
And He that lives, this Same is He that dies.'—
'Then here is myrrh: alas! yea woe is me
That myrrh befitteth Thee.'—

Myrrh, frankincense, and gold:
And lo! from wintry fold
Good-will doth bring
A Lamb, the innocent likeness of this King
Whom stars and seraphs sing:
    And lo! the bird of love, a Dove,
    Flutters and coos above:
    And Dove and Lamb and Babe agree in love:—
Come all mankind, come all creation hither,
Come, worship Christ together.

The place of the magi in the Nativity narrative is complex and
problematic. They have been represented as being present at the
Nativity, yet equally as arriving up to two years after Christ's
birth. In the popular devotional mind there are three, all kings,
and yet – as all biblical scholars know – the text of Matthew
does not specify the number of magi, only the number of gifts.
They have been given names and had traditions attached to
them; they have been seen as astrologers and astronomers and
as believers in a strange religion. They have acted as the great
Other in the Nativity stories and yet as agents of God. They
are key actors in what many people see as the culminating
feast of Christmas, the Epiphany – the manifestation of Christ
– and as stand-ins for all of us who cannot claim a place in the
Jewish story of salvation. The feast of the Epiphany represents
the manifestation to the Gentiles, to the outsiders, to us. The
magi – like so many of us – have been drawn in by God's pull
towards the centre, only to be sent out into the world changed.
    The first three stanzas of 'Epiphany' ostensibly take the
form of dialogues between the three magi and whom? Christ,
God, an angel? The Spirit? Certainly, it is a voice that speaks

on behalf of the divine, perhaps registered in the internal self-narrative of each magi. For as the magi draw close to the infant-Christ, each comes with an entirely reasonable question or concern, a concern that – of course – is ultimately ours. As the gold-bearing magi asks, if Christ be a king, 'Where is Thy court?' There is a perversity in Christianity that insists the King of Creation is not to be found in palace or court; or perhaps better, the court is found outside our human conceptions of glory. As the poem suggests, 'This Infant of a span / Is He man sought for since the world began!' In Christ, all conceptions of kingship are overturned and gold – power's symbol – is never worthy enough. And yet, still the magi – and we – leaves their gift.

The questions, of course, do not end there. The magi who bears a token of priestly authority – frankincense – asks, 'But wherefore dost Thou keep so mean a state, / Low-lying desolate?' This gesture towards Christ's priestly authority not only underlines the questions about the nature of his kingship, but actually takes us further into the mystery: if Christ is Great High Priest, should he not be the minister at the mysteries of the Temple, clothed in ephod and fine raiment? His altar, however, is not only humble, but will ultimately entail the sacrifice of himself. For this is no stand-in for God, but God himself. He *is* the Holy of Holies: 'The Lord our God is here / Approachable, Who bids us all draw near.' Rather than being sealed off from us in mystery and high terror, the God who is born is approachable; this ironic god displays his omnipotence in vulnerable flesh. This, of course, gestures towards death and its symbol: myrrh, that strange token of sacrifice and death. The third magi says, 'Then here is myrrh: alas! yea woe is me / That myrrh befitteth Thee', and the voice of the divine reminds us, 'He that lives, this Same is He that dies.'

When Rossetti invites us, in a conventional way, to 'Come all mankind, come all creation hither, / Come, worship Christ together', she does so with a tempered sentiment. For if in the final stanza the poem deploys familiar and overly sentimentalized images of Christ – 'lamb', 'dove' – it is in the context of a rich and complex understanding of gold, frankincense and myrrh; these three symbols push us out of our cosy ideas of Christ. The unsentimental horizons of these symbols expose our presuppositions and established positions. For if we want God to be comfortable in the halls of gold, and the scented courts of the Cathedral and Temple, we are less sure that we are prepared to anoint him for death. God occupies all of those spaces, but in a subversive way: his Kingdom is a hovel, his Temple is his body, his life is his death and his death is life. He shows us what we need even if it is not what we want. He brings us, at this culmination of the Christmas feast, back to the facts of God. Rossetti's poem challenges us to worship him as he is: as the King of Glory whose glory is vulnerable humanity transformed. He calls us out from our temples and palaces – literal and metaphorical – to gather around the infant like those first magi, and be transformed and transfixed in wonder.

Postscript: Candlemas

Our grapes fresh from the vine,
Pomegranates full and fine,
Dates and sharp bullaces,
Rare pears and greengages,
Damsons and bilberries,
Taste them and try:
Currants and gooseberries,
Bright-fire-like barberries,
Figs to fill your mouth,
Citrons from the South,
Sweet to tongue and sound to eye;
Come buy, come buy.

If you have stuck with this book so far, I trust that – as you read the words above from 'Goblin Market' – there is a sense in which you approach them with fresh eyes. This book began with the double-edged invitation – modelled so clearly by our contemporary approaches to Advent and Christmas – to 'come buy, come buy'. I hope that the encounter with Rossetti's poetry offered in this book has enriched, interrogated and unfolded richer themes than those presented by the often tempting, mouth-watering, but ultimately tasteless 'fruits' of a consumer culture. I hope too that her poetic readings of Advent, Christmas and winter seem both less strange and yet stranger still than one might have supposed at the outset.

I know that some will be surprised, or disappointed, or perhaps even relieved that I chose to end this book for Advent and Christmas on the feast of the Epiphany. I know only too well that for many the season of Christmas extends through to Candlemas, or the Feast of the Presentation, on 2 February. I do not want to discourage anyone from keeping the Christmas feast until that date, and I belong to a tradition that shall keep its crib scenes in place until Candlemas. However, for the sake of focus, as well as time and space constraints, I am at ease with the editorial decision I make to end this book at Epiphany. At the same time, here is one more poem for the reader to consider.[27] It gives us the opportunity to rehearse many of the themes more broadly considered in this book, as well as closing where I began, with the theme of 'fruit' or 'fruitfulness'.

Feast of the Presentation

O Firstfruits of our grain,
Infant and Lamb appointed to be slain,
A Virgin and two doves were all Thy train,
With one old man for state,
When Thou didst enter first Thy Father's gate.

Since then Thy train hath been
Freeman and bondman, bishop, king and queen,
With flaming candles and with garlands green:
Oh happy all who wait
One day or thousand days around Thy gate.

And these have offered Thee,
Beside their hearts, great stores for charity,
Gold, frankincense, and myrrh; if such may be
For savour or for state
Within the threshold of Thy golden gate.

Then snowdrops and my heart
I'll bring, to find those blacker than Thou art:
Yet, loving Lord, accept us in good part;
And give me grace to wait,
A bruised reed bowed low before Thy gate.

Candlemas, or the Presentation, celebrated 40 days after Christmas Day, is seen as the culmination of the Christmas feast. It is grounded in the story found in Luke 2, where 40 days after Christ's birth Mary and Joseph take their firstborn to the Temple to present him to God and make a sacrifice of dedication and thanksgiving. It is during this visit that an old man named Simeon proclaims Jesus as the Christ using the famous words known as the *Nunc Dimittis*: 'Lord, now let your servant depart in peace, according to your word; for my eyes have seen your salvation which you have prepared in the presence of all peoples, a light for revelation to the Gentiles, and for glory to your people Israel.' An old woman, Anna the prophetess, also sings a song in honour of Christ.

This poem presents Christ as the 'Firstfruits of our grain'. The reader is reminded that – when placed alongside the empty fruits of the goblin men in 'Goblin Market' – this is fruit that shall satisfy; it shall be drunk/eaten and shall feed. As such it gestures – when placed alongside the lamb that shall be sacrificed – to the central Christian ritual meal, the Eucharist. Indeed, one of the outstanding features of Rossetti's poem is the way it gestures towards the ritual and the liturgical. Its opening stanza, which features a simple cast of characters, reminds the reader that from those simple origins a whole panoply of peoples have stood in witness to the Living God:

Since then Thy train hath been
Freeman and bondman, bishop, king and queen,
With flaming candles and with garlands green:
Oh happy all who wait
One day or thousand days around Thy gate.

This grand train is reminiscent of the comments of a more recent poet, U. A. Fanthorpe, who in 'Getting It Across' makes unflattering and amusing comments about those in whom Christ has entrusted his message of hope and grace. In Rossetti's case I do not sense any side or sneer. Rather, there is a sense of awe in the way that all walks of life have been called to the Flame of

Christ – from free to slave, from humble to the most exalted. The simple ceremony of the original Presentation of Jesus to his Father, 40 days after his birth, has been transmuted into a great festival of light and garlands. This is a place of rejoicing.

Appropriately enough, the final stanza echoes that found in the poem from which this book takes its title. It has Rossetti's characteristic humility and simplicity and reminds the reader that behind the rejoicing and the 'great stores of charity', anyone may make their offering:

> Then snowdrops and my heart
> I'll bring, to find those blacker than Thou art:
> Yet, loving Lord, accept us in good part;
> And give me grace to wait,
> A bruised reed bowed low before Thy gate.

It is a plea for generosity and grace; it is a plea for others and for the speaker herself. It shows the speaker in solidarity with Simeon and Anna. It is, as I trust this book's readers have come to expect, Rossetti demonstrating her solidarity with her fellow pilgrims, bruised reeds that we all are. It is a request that all people of faith are invited to make: a request for sufficient grace to wait for the Lord in our predicament, our absurdity, our beauty and foolishness. For soon, and very soon, it shall be Advent and Christmas again. Soon, our Lord shall come in judgement and grace to transform the whole of the universe into the Kingdom that was and is and is yet to come.

Appendix: Some Other Poems

I am conscious that there are a number of poems I would have liked to have had space to discuss in this book, as well as the fact that Advent is a season that can last up to 28 days; this book contains meditations for just 24. These twin considerations have led me to offer a short selection of 'other' Rossetti poems that might be slotted into additional days of Advent in coming years or offer alternative points of meditation in any given year. There are, in addition, other poems that are suitable for Advent and Christmas and wintry meditation. I encourage the reader to seek them out by acquiring a collection like *The Complete Poems of Christina Rossetti* (London: Penguin Classics, 2005 (2001)).

I Dug and Dug

I dug and dug amongst the snow,
And though the flowers would never grow;
I dug and dug amongst the sand,
And still no green thing came to hand.

Melt, O snow! the warm winds blow
To thaw the flowers and melt the snow;
But all the winds from every land
Will rear no blossom from the sand.

Amor Mundi

'Oh, where are you going with your love-locks flowing
On the west wind blowing along this valley track?'
'The downhill path is easy, come with me an' it please ye,
We shall escape the uphill by never turning back.'

So they two went together in glowing August weather,
The honey-breathing heather lay to their left and right;
And dear she was to doat on, her swift feet seemed to float
    on
The air like soft twin pigeons too sportive to alight.

'Oh, what is that in heaven where grey cloud-flakes are
    seven,
Where blackest clouds hang riven just at the rainy skirt?'
'Oh, that's a meteor sent us, a message dumb, portentous,
An undeciphered solemn signal of help or hurt.'

'Oh, what is that glides quickly where velvet flowers grow
    thickly,
Their scent comes rich and sickly?'—'A scaled and hooded
    worm.'
'Oh, what's that in the hollow, so pale I quake to follow?'
'Oh, that's a thin dead body which waits the eternal term.'

'Turn again, O my sweetest,—turn again, false and fleetest:
This beaten way whereof thou beatest I fear is hell's own
    track.'
'Nay, too steep for hill-mounting; nay, too late for cost-
    counting:
This downhill path is easy, but there's no turning back.'

Balm in Gilead

Heartsease I found, where Love-lies-bleeding
   Empurpled all the ground:
Whatever flowers I missed unheeding,
   Heartsease I found.

   Yet still my garden mound
Stood sore in need of watering, weeding,
   And binding growths unbound.

Ah, when shades fell to light succeeding
I scarcely dared look round:
'Love-lies-bleeding' was all my pleading,
Heartsease I found.

Vigil of the Annunciation[28]

All weareth, all wasteth,
All flitteth, all hasteth,
All of flesh and time:—
Sound, sweet heavenly chime,
Ring in the unutterable eternal prime.

Man hopeth, man feareth,
Man droopeth:—Christ cheereth,
Compassing release,
Comforting with peace,
Promising rest where strife and anguish cease.

Saints waking, saints sleeping,
Rest well in safe keeping;
Well they rest today
While they watch and pray
But their tomorrow's rest what tongue shall say?

Feast of the Annunciation

Whereto shall we liken this Blessed Mary Virgin,
Faithful shoot from Jesse's root graciously emerging?
Lily we might call her, but Christ alone is white;
Rose delicious, but that Jesus is the one Delight;
Flower of women, but her Firstborn is mankind's one
    flower:
He the Sun lights up all moons thro' their radiant hour.
'Blessed among women, highly favoured,' thus
Glorious Gabriel hailed her, teaching words to us:
Whom devoutly copying we too cry 'All hail!'
Echoing on the music of glorious Gabriel.

Herself a rose, who bore the Rose,
    She bore the Rose and felt its thorn.
    All Loveliness new-born
Took on her bosom its repose,
    And slept and woke there night and morn.

Lily herself, she bore the one
    Fair Lily; sweeter, whiter, far
    Than she or others are:
The Sun of Righteousness her Son,
    She was His morning star.

She gracious, He essential Grace,
    He was the Fountain, she the rill:
    Her goodness to fulfil
And gladness, with proportioned pace
    He led her steps thro' good and ill.

Christ's mirror she of grace and love,
    Of beauty and of life and death:
    By hope and love and faith
Transfigured to His Likeness, 'Dove,
    Spouse, Sister, Mother,' Jesus saith.

Golden Holly

Common Holly bears a berry
To make Christmas Robins merry:—
Golden Holly bears a rose,
Unfolding at October's close
To cheer an old Friend's eyes and nose.

But Give Me Holly, Bold and Jolly

A Rose has thorns as well as honey,
I'll not have her for love or money;
An iris grows so straight and fine
That she shall be no friend of mine;
Snowdrops like the snow would chill me;
Nightshade would caress and kill me;
Crocus like a spear would fright me;
Dragon's-mouth might bark or bite me;
Convolvulus but blooms to die;
A wind-flower suggests a sigh;
Love-lies-bleeding makes me sad;
And poppy-juice would drive me mad:—
But give me holly, bold and jolly,
Honest, prickly, shining holly;
Pluck me holly leaf and berry
For the day when I make merry.

Hail! Noble Face of Noble Friend

Hail, noble face of noble friend!—
    Hail, honoured master hand and dear!—
On you may Christmas good descend
    And blessings of the unknown year
    So soon to overtake us here.
Unknown, yet well known: I portend
Love starts the course, love seals the end.

St. John, the Apostle

'Beloved, let us love one another,' says St. John,
   Eagle of eagles calling from above:
Words of strong nourishment for life to feed upon,
   'Beloved, let us love.'

   Voice of an eagle, yea, Voice of the Dove:
If we may love, winter is past and gone;
   Publish we, praise we, for lo it is enough.

More sunny than sunshine that ever yet shone,
   Sweetener of the bitter, smoother of the rough,
Highest lesson of all lessons for all to con,
   'Beloved, let us love.'

Holy Innocents

Sleep, little Baby, sleep,
   The holy Angels love thee,
And guard thy bed, and keep
   A blessed watch above thee.
No spirit can come near
   Nor evil beast to harm thee;
Sleep, Sweet, devoid of fear
   Where nothing need alarm thee.

The Love which doth not sleep,
   The eternal arms around thee;
The shepherd of the sheep
   In perfect love has found thee.
Sleep through the holy night,
   Christ-kept from snare and sorrow,
Until thou wake to light
   And love and warmth to-morrow.

January Cold Desolate

January cold desolate;
February all dripping wet;
March wind ranges;
April changes;
Birds sing in tune
  To flowers of May,
And sunny June
  Brings longest day;
In scorched July
The storm-clouds fly
Lightning torn;
August bears corn,
September fruit;
In rough October
Earth must disrobe her;
Stars fall and shoot
In keen November;
And night is long
And cold is strong
In bleak December.

All Saints

They have brought gold and spices to my King,
  Incense and precious stuffs and ivory;
O holy Mother mine, what can I bring
  That so my Lord may deign to look on me?
They sing a sweeter song than I can sing,
  All crowned and glorified exceedingly:
I, bound on earth, weep for my trespassing—
  They sing the song of love in Heaven, set free.
Then answered me my Mother, and her voice
  Spake to my heart, yea answered in my heart:

Sing, saith He to the Heavens, to Earth, Rejoice:
Thou also lift thy heart to Him above:
 He seeks not thine, but thee such as thou art,
For lo His banner over thee is Love.

Epiphanytide

Trembling before Thee we fall down to adore Thee,
 Shamefaced and trembling we lift our eyes to Thee:
O First and with the last! annul our ruined past,
 Rebuild us to Thy glory, set us free
 From sin and from sorrow to fall down and worship
 Thee.

Full of pity view us, stretch Thy sceptre to us,
 Bid us live that we may give ourselves to Thee:
O faithful Lord and True! stand up for us and do,
 Make us lovely, make us new, set us free—
 Heart and soul and spirit—to bring all and worship
 Thee.

Vigil of the Presentation

Long and dark the nights, dim and short the days,
Mounting weary heights on our weary ways,
 Thee our God we praise.
Scaling heavenly heights by unearthly ways,
Thee our God we praise all our nights and days,
 Thee our God we praise.

The Purification of St. Mary The Virgin

Purity born of a Maid:
Was such a Virgin defiled?
Nay, by no shade of a shade.
She offered her gift of pure love,
A dove with a fair fellow-dove,
She offered her Innocent Child
The Essence and Author of Love;
The Lamb that indwelt by the Dove
Was spotless and holy and mild;
More pure than all other,
More pure than His Mother,
Her God and Redeemer and Child.

A Candlemas Dialogue

'Love brought Me down: and cannot love make thee
Carol for joy to Me?
Hear cheerful robin carol from his tree,
Who owes not half to Me
I won for thee.'

'Yea, Lord, I hear his carol's wordless voice;
And well may he rejoice
Who hath not heard of death's discordant noise.
So might I too rejoice
With such a voice.'

'True, thou hast compassed death: but hast not thou
The tree of life's own bough?
Am I not Life and Resurrection now?
My Cross balm-bearing bough
For such as thou.'

'Ah me, Thy Cross!—but that seems far away;
Thy Cradle-song today
I too would raise and worship Thee and pray:
Not empty, Lord, today
Send me away.'

'If thou wilt not go empty, spend thy store;
And I will give thee more,
Yea, make thee ten times richer than before.
Give more and give yet more
Out of thy store.'

'Because Thou givest me Thyself, I will
Thy blessed word fulfil,
Give with both hands, and hoard by giving still:
Thy pleasure to fulfil,
And work Thy Will.'

Selected Bibliography

Armstrong, Isobel, 'Anna Letitia Barbauld: A Unitarian Poetics?', in *Anna Letitia Barbauld: New Perspectives*, ed. by William McCarthy and Olivia Murphy (Lewisburg, PA: Bucknell University Press, 2014), pp. 59–82.

——, *Victorian Poetry: Poetry, Poetics and Politics* (London: Routledge, 1993).

Arseneau, Mary, 'Incarnation and Interpretation: Christina Rossetti, the Oxford Movement, and "Goblin Market"', *Victorian Poetry*, 31.1 (1993), 79–93.

——, *Recovering Christina Rossetti: Female Community and Incarnational Poetics* (Basingstoke: Palgrave Macmillan, 2004).

Arseneau, Mary, Antony H. Harrison, and Lorraine Janzen Kooistra, eds, *The Culture of Christina Rossetti: Female Poetics and Victorian Contexts* (Athens, OH: Ohio University Press, 1999).

Avery, Simon, 'Christina Rossetti: Gender and Power', British Library, (2015) [accessed 03/01/2019].

Bristow, Joseph, ed., *The Victorian Poet: Poetics and Persona* (London: Routledge, 1987).

Brown, Susan, 'The Victorian Poetess', in *The Cambridge Companion to Victorian Poetry*, ed. by Joseph Bristow (Cambridge: Cambridge University Press, 2000), pp. 180–202.

Byron, Glennis, 'Rethinking the Dramatic Monologue: Victorian Women Poets and Social Critique', in *Victorian Women Poets*, ed. by Alison Chapman (Cambridge: Brewer, 2003), pp. 79–98.

D'Amico, Diane, '"Choose the stairs that mount above": Christina Rossetti and the Anglican Sisterhoods', *Essays in Literature*, 17.2 (1990), 204–21.

——, *Christina Rossetti: Faith, Gender, and Time* (Baton Rouge, LA: Louisiana State University Press, 1999).

D'Amico, Diane, and David A. Kent, 'Rossetti and the Tractarians', *Victorian Poetry*, 44.1 (2006), 93–104.

Dieleman, Karen, *Religious Imaginaries: The Liturgical and Poetic Practices of Elizabeth Barrett Browning, Christina Rossetti, and Adelaide Procter* (Athens, OH: Ohio University Press, 2012).

Harrison, Antony H., 'Christina Rossetti: Illness and Ideology', *Victorian Poetry*, 45.4 (2007), 415–28.

Hassett, Constance W., *Christina Rossetti: The Patience of Style* (Charlottesville, VA and London: University of Virginia Press, 2005).

Helsinger, Elizabeth K., 'Consumer Power and the Utopia of Desire: Christina Rossetti's "Goblin Market"', *ELH*, 58.4 (1991), 903–33.

Herringer, Carol Engelhardt, *Victorians and the Virgin Mary: Religion and Gender in England, 1830–85, Gender in History* (Manchester: Manchester University Press, 2014).

Hill, Marylu, '"Eat Me, Drink Me, Love Me": Eucharist and the Erotic Body in Christina Rossetti's "Goblin Market"', *Victorian Poetry*, 43.4 (2005), 455–72.

Hu, Esther T., 'Christina Rossetti, John Keble, and the Divine Gaze', *Victorian Poetry*, 46.2 (2008), 175–89.

Jones, Timothy Willem, *Sexual Politics in the Church of England, 1857–1957* (Oxford: Oxford University Press, 2013).

Lane, Belden C., *The Solace of Fierce Landscapes* (Oxford: Oxford University Press, 2007).

Lootens, Tricia A., *Lost Saints: Silence, Gender, and Victorian Literary Canonization* (Charlottesville, VA and London: University of Virginia Press, 1996).

Ludlow, Elizabeth, *Christina Rossetti and the Bible: Waiting with the Saints* (London and New York: Bloomsbury, 2014).

Lysack, Krista, *Come Buy, Come Buy: Shopping and the Culture of Consumption in Victorian Women's Writing* (Athens, OH: Ohio University Press, 2008).

——, 'The Production of Time: Keble, Rossetti, and Victorian Devotional Reading', *Victorian Studies*, 55.3 (2013), 451–70.

Marsh, Jan, *Christina Rossetti: A Literary Biography* (London: Cape, 1994).

Mason, Emma, 'Christina Rossetti and the Doctrine of Reserve', *Journal of Victorian Culture*, 7.2 (2002), 196–219.

——, *Christina Rossetti: Poetry, Ecology, Faith (Spiritual Lives)* (Oxford: Oxford University Press, 2018).

——, 'Tractarian Poetry: Introduction', *Victorian Poetry*, 44.1 (2006), 1–6.

Palazzo, Lynda, *Christina Rossetti's Feminist Theology* (Basingstoke and New York: Palgrave, 2002).

Pearsall, Cornelia D. J., 'The Dramatic Monologue', in *The Cambridge Companion to Victorian Poetry*, ed. by Joseph Bristow (Cambridge: Cambridge University Press, 2000), pp. 67–88.

Rappoport, Jill, *Giving Women: Alliance and Exchange in Victorian Culture* (Oxford: Oxford University Press, 2012).

Rose, Gillian, *Love's Work* (London: Chatto & Windus, 1995).

Rossetti, Christina, *The Complete Poems* (London: Penguin, 2005 (2001)).

Slinn, E. Warwick, 'Dramatic Monologue', in *A Companion to Victorian Poetry*, ed. by Richard Cronin, Alison Chapman and Antony H. Harrison (Oxford: Blackwell, 2007 (2002)), pp. 80–98.

Thomas, Frances, *Christina Rossetti* (Hanley Swan: The Self Publishing Association, 1992).

Notes

1 Careful readers will note an inconsistency here. Generally, I shall follow modern convention by using the single word 'midwinter' in this book. However, Rossetti herself hyphenates the word in the original poem. I have kept her form intact when quoting from 'A Christmas Carol' directly.

2 Indeed, as I've suggested among others, in 'Goblin Market' Lizzie's offering of her own body to her dying sister Laura as a token of salvation offers an early feminist reading of a female Christ figure:

Come and kiss me.
Never mind my bruises,
Hug me, kiss me, suck my juices
Squeez'd from goblin fruits for you,
Goblin pulp and goblin dew.
Eat me, drink me, love me;
Laura, make much of me;
For your sake I have braved the glen
And had to do with goblin merchant men.
Laura started from her chair,
Flung her arms up in the air,
Clutch'd her hair:
'Lizzie, Lizzie, have you tasted
For my sake the fruit forbidden?
Must your light like mine be hidden,
Your young life like mine be wasted,
Undone in mine undoing,
And ruin'd in my ruin,
Thirsty, canker'd, goblin-ridden?'—
She clung about her sister,
Kiss'd and kiss'd and kiss'd her:
Tears once again
Refresh'd her shrunken eyes,
Dropping like rain
After long sultry drouth;
Shaking with aguish fear, and pain ...

3 Recent books that take the religious dimensions of Rossetti's poetry seriously include: Karen Dieleman, *Religious Imaginaries: The Liturgical and Poetic Practices of Elizabeth Barrett Browning, Christina Rossetti, and Adelaide Procter* (Athens, OH: Ohio University Press, 2012); F. Elizabeth Gray, *Christian and Lyric Tradition in Victorian Women's Poetry* (New York and Abingdon: Routledge, 2014 (2010)); Lynda Palazzo, *Christina Rossetti's Feminist Theology* (Basingstoke and New York: Palgrave, 2002); Elizabeth Ludlow, *Christina Rossetti and the Bible: Waiting with the Saints* (London and New York: Bloomsbury, 2014).

4 The critic Mary Arseneau has argued that John Keble's poetics suggest that Christ's incarnation acts as the meeting point of this world and the next. She then argues that Rossetti's poetry effectively takes this idea to the next level; in effect, it embodies Keble's idea about the incarnation. Rossetti's poetry is not simply about pointing beyond this life, but in grounding flourishing Christian community in this life. Christ acts as the incarnational fulcrum to which serious human living – ethical and spiritual – orientates. Just as Tractarian 'reserve' demands that the believer be cautious in their theological pronouncements on the nature of God and doctrine and the Church (as Christ himself was reserved), so a Tractarian poetics should be marked by reserve, allusion and restraint. Only thereby can poetry be the faithful handmaid of theology. In a recent *Church Times* review of Emma Mason's superb book on Rossetti and ecology, *Christina Rossetti: Poetry, Ecology, Faith*, Suzanne Fagence Cooper says, 'Keble, Pusey, and Newman all privileged poetry as an art that could conjure the "world out of sight", and represent the intercommunion of all Creation.' The notion of 'reserve' as the unfolding of divine truth gradually, delightfully seems particularly relevant with Rossetti. As shall become apparent, Rossetti so often exemplifies Keble's ideal, crafting poetry at once 'fervent yet sober … neither wild and passionate, nor light and airy'.

5 Not least because time in the European medieval era was constructed around the hours kept by the professionally Religious as much as around the patterns of nature; the emergence of the town clock, and then the watch in the early modern and modern eras, reconstructed time again.

6 Rossetti writes several poems titled 'Advent', just as she writes a number of poems called 'A Christmas Carol'. I shall add in the date of composition to distinguish between poems.

7 An early poem, 'In an Artist's Studio', written in 1856 but only published after her death, brings out the tense artistic and gendered questions at stake in Rossetti's poetry:

One face looks out from all his canvases,
One selfsame figure sits or walks or leans;

We found her hidden just behind those screens,
That mirror gave back all her loveliness.
A queen in opal or in ruby dress,

A nameless girl in freshest summer-greens,
A saint, an angel—every canvas means
The same one meaning, neither more nor less.
He feeds upon her face by day and night,

And she with true kind eyes looks back on him,
Fair as the moon and joyful as the light:
Not wan with waiting, not with sorrow dim;
Not as she is, but as when hope shone bright;
Not as she is, but as she fills his dream.

'In an Artist's Studio' is a Petrarchan rather than Shakespearean sonnet, using a classic *abbaabbacdcdcd* rhyme scheme. The Petrarchan form perhaps only underlines Rossetti's critical strategy in the poem, for – unlike Shakespeare's variant – the Petrarchan form works well as a means of constructing an 'argument'. Classically, the opening octave (*abbaabba*) serves to set up the argument or proposition of the poem, while the closing twin tercets or sestet serves to offer a resolution. Within this structure the volta in the ninth line presents 'a turn' in the argument. The sonnet form is traditionally the poem of love. What 'In an Artist's Studio' offers, however, is an insight into the feminist edge present in Rossetti's poetry: for it constitutes a cutting critique of the ways in which the female model – William Michael Rossetti suggested she might be based on the Pre-Raphaelite muse Elizabeth Siddal – is painted, 'framed' and controlled by the male artist.

The critic Simon Avery offers a powerful summary of the tensions and issues at stake in this poem:

On looking round the studio, the speaker is appalled by the reductive similarity of all the paintings, the single vision of the artist caught in the repeated use of the word 'one' – '[o]ne face', '[o]ne selfsame figure', 'same one meaning'. The model's actual identity is lost and she is subsequently reconstructed as various female icons ('queen', 'saint', 'angel') or as a 'nameless girl'. Indeed, the idea of the model being at the mercy of the artist's whims is reinforced at the beginning of the sonnet's sestet, where the artist appears as a kind of vampire figure who 'feeds upon her face by day and night' (l.9). The model is drained of life, the poem suggests, so that the artist can gratify his fantasies. Indeed, time and again in Rossetti's poems, the female figure is depicted as entrapped or confined – physically, psychologically or both.

'In an Artist's Studio' suggests that the 'saint' in the picture is as fixed by the male gaze as the Blessed Virgin ever was. The artist makes a dream woman for himself. She exists to look only on the artist who made her, not at herself or at the world. She embodies – as queen, as saint, as angel – 'The same one meaning, neither more nor less'.

8 Emma Mason, *Christina Rossetti: Poetry, Ecology, Faith (Spiritual Lives)* (Oxford: Oxford University Press, 2018).

9 Diane D'Amico, *Christina Rossetti: Faith, Gender and Time* (Baton Rouge, LA: Louisiana State University, 1999), p. 34.

10 E. Warwick Slinn, 'Dramatic Monologue', in *A Companion to Victorian Poetry*, ed. by Richard Cronin, Alison Chapman and Antony H. Harrison (Oxford: Blackwell, 2007 (2002)), pp. 80–98 (p. 80).

11 Glennis Byron, 'Rethinking the Dramatic Monologue: Victorian Women Poets and Social Critique', in *Victorian Women Poets*, ed. by Alison Chapman (Cambridge: Brewer), pp. 79–98 (p. 80). As Byron notes, the arguments of Herbert F. Tucker have been significant for the 'standard' position – see, especially, Herbert F. Tucker, 'From Monomania to Monologue: "St Simeon Stylites" and the Rise of the Victorian Dramatic Monologue', *Victorian Poetry*, 22.2 (1984), 121–37; Herbert F. Tucker, 'Dramatic Monologue and the Overhearing of Lyric', in *Lyric Poetry: Beyond New Criticism*, ed. by Chaviva Hosek and Patricia Parker (Ithaca, NY: Cornell University Press, 1985), pp. 226–43.

12 See, especially, Isobel Armstrong, *Victorian Poetry: Poetry, Poetics and Politics* (London: Routledge, 1993), pp. 318–22.

13 Pindar, Nemean VIII, 40–2, translated by Martha Nussbaum in *The Fragility of Goodness* (Cambridge: Cambridge University Press, 1986), p. 1.

14 Lizzie Ludlow, *Christina Rossetti and the Bible: Waiting with the Saints* (London and New York: Bloomsbury, 2014), p. 63.

15 For example, Rachel Mann, *Fierce Imaginings* (London: Darton, Longman and Todd, 2017).

16 *Dwelling in Possibility: Women Poets and Critics on Poetry*, ed. by Yopie Prins and Maeera Shrieber (Ithaca, NY and London: Cornell University Press, 1997), p. 1.

17 This is the evocative phrase of the late poet Les Murray, when describing the poetry of Michael Symmons Roberts.

18 Psalm 121 is part of the Song of Ascents, sometimes known as the Pilgrim Songs. This section of the psalms covers numbers 120 to 134. It is commonly believed that these psalms were sung by worshippers as they ascended the road to Jerusalem for the great Jewish festivals.

19 Belden C. Lane, *The Solace of Fierce Landscapes* (Oxford: Oxford University Press, 2007).

20 I have taken a liberty in separating this poem from its twin 'Advent', used in this book as the poem for Advent Four. In *Verses*, these poems appeared as a pair, separated by a largish block of empty

page; each poem strikes me as holding its own unique power and consistency. I hope readers shall indulge my editorial judgement here.

21 Constance W. Hassett, *Christina Rossetti: The Patience of Style* (Charlottesville, VA and London: University of Virginia Press, 2005), p. 59.

22 Hassett, *Christina Rossetti*.

23 Hassett, *Christina Rossetti*, p. 63.

24 The phrase 'Octave of Christmas' may be unfamiliar to some readers, especially those who fall outside of Catholic traditions. The term, referring to an eight-day period of prayer or feasting, gained traction in both the Western and the Eastern Churches from the fourth century onwards. The eight days offer the worshipper a full week of prayerful devotion and focus.

25 As Hilary Mantel reminds us at the end of *Wolf Hall*, in large parts of medieval Europe the official New Year began on 25 March, Lady Day. That progressive trading centre, the City-State of Venice, signalled the shift to starting the official New Year on 1 January. As Mantel writes, 'England did not catch up till 1752.'

26 This stanza references the famous prayer of St Richard of Chichester. It also formed the basis of the song 'Day By Day' from the musical *Godspell*.

27 Should you wish to read some more poems suitable for Advent/ Christmas and/or winter, please turn to the Appendix on page 158. Alternatively, plunge further into Rossetti's oeuvre. There are countless treasures to be discovered.

28 I am aware that the feast of the Annunciation is held on 25 March. However, the following poems may be especially suitable for those wishing to meditate, during Advent, on the place of Mary as the God-Bearer, or *Theotokos*, especially around the Fourth Sunday of Advent.